john r. mabry

God is a Great Underground River

articles, essays & homilies
on interfaith spirituality

the apocryphile press
BERKELEY, CA
www.apocryphile.org

Apocryphile Press
1700 Shattuck Ave #81
Berkeley, CA 94709
www.apocryphile.org

"An End to Suffering," "Are We Just Born Bad?," "As Below, So Above," "Bede Griffiths: Holy Man for Our Time," "Bear Each Others' Burdens," "Courage for Creative Theology," "Each in Their Own Tongue," "God the Heretic," "Hindu Myth and Paradigm Shift," "More Than Men," "Morality and Work," "Ritual: Religion in Action," "Second-Guessing God," "The God that Stands By," "The Sacrificed God," "Teilhard de Chardin and the Formation of the Noosphere," "There is No Salvation (Apart from the Body)," and "Who Do You Trust? (The Issue of Spiritual Authority)" were originally published in *Creation Spirituality* magazine.

"Apocalypse Now?" was originally published in the inaugural issue of *The Ferret*.

"A Companion on the Journey: Interfaith Spiritual Direction," was originally published in an abridged form in the Newsletter of the Chaplaincy Institute for Arts and Interfaith Ministry.

"The Way of Non-Direction: Insights on Spiritual Direction from the Tao Te Ching," was originally published in *Presence: An International Journal of Spiritual Direction*.

"False Self and Original Nature: Reflections from Suzuki and Merton," "Fundamentalism: Making Peace with the Prophets of Doom," "Hsün Tzu and Augustine of Hippo," "Strange Bedfellows: Hinduism and Judaic Mysticism in Comparison," "Two Eyes, One Object: A Comparison of Dieties as Found in the Bhagavad-Gita and the Poetry of Jelaluddin Rumi," "Process Thought and the Hopi Universe," and "That Naughty Bishop of Hippo: Dysfunctional Theological Innovations of St. Augustine" were written as part of graduate studies at the California Institute of Integral Studies.

"Christian Heresies in the East" was originally delivered at the Cultural Integration Fellowship in San Francisco, CA.

"A Matter of Perspective," "Festivals of Light: Hanukkah & Christmas," "Power—the Greatest Temptation," and "The Primal Spiritual Process," were sermons delivered at Grace North Church; "Krishna: The Lover of Our Souls" was delivered at Unity of Clearlake; "God Belongs to Everyone," was delivered at an ordination service of the Chaplaincy Institute for Arts and Interfaith Ministry.

"Magic: Mysticism or Manipulation?" was written specifically for this collection.

Contents

Introduction

When I first began to study religious traditions other than my own, my mother became distraught. "You'll become confused," she objected, meaning that she was afraid that I would forsake the truth of Christianity if my mind were filled with so many "heretical ideas."

I do understand her reticence. To honestly exchange ideas means to set aside, even if momentarily, the assumption that *I am right*. This, for some Christians, is very threatening. To think for a moment that a faith tradition other than my own might merit study flies in the face of the historical church's exclusive claims. To admit that there might be some truth in Buddhism, for example, seems to contradict Jesus' assertion that he is the "way, the truth, and the light." There are many ways to approach this "problem," and many fine books have been written attempting to reconcile the exclusive claims of Christ with a pluralistic sensability. This is not one of these august texts. This book assumes that Jesus is indeed "the way, the truth, and the light"—for Christians. Muslims and Buddhists have lights of their own.

I have discovered that no matter what tradition you explore, you find a God that is relentless, irrepresible; a God who desires to be in relationship with human beings, who calls for us to live in harmony with Creation. God has not just chosen the Jews, nor the Christians. God has chosen every people, and the Spirit has spoken in every age and on every continent, "each in their own tongue." Meister Eckhart in the thirteenth century gave us an image of just this sort of God, when he said "God is a great underground river that cannot be dammed up."

In a favorite story of mine of Sufi origin this image is echoed. The Sufi master comes upon a man who has been dabbling a little bit with Christianity, a little bit with Islam, trying this and that, but not making any real commitments in his spiritual life. The master counsels his disciple "Don't go around, digging shallow holes here and there, trying out this and that. Pick one spot. Dig deep. You will hit water." God is a great underground river, and each of our great traditions has a well.

The reflections which follow sample and compare the waters drawn from these wells. You may call them exploration into "Deep Ecumenism," the title of the irregular column published in *Creation Spirituality* magazine where many of them first appeared, in that they propose to find the deep unity of the Spirit as it appears both in the Chrsitian tradition and in her wondrous sister traditions. You may call them works of "speculative theology," in that they are presented not as doctrine, much less dogma, but as mere meditations for one's consideration. Here I choose to call them *God is a Great Underground River*, for their mysterious and common source. They are an invitation to dream, to stretch, to begin to reach out in friendship with our imaginations, and to share the vision of the Holy as seen through other eyes.

After many years, I can look back and say that it is true that my study of other faith traditions has changed me. It has done many things for me, but confusing me is not among them. They have, instead, inspired me, and enriched my spiritual life beyond measure. As for my mother's fear of heresy, I have come to the conclusion that it is God who is the greatest heretic, unconcerned with any one group's dogma or constraints. God, the great underground river, will not be dammed up. Neither our dogmas, nor our creeds or decrees will keep back this torrent. No priestly pronouncement will check the Spirit's progress. No government, no church, no leader can stop it. The divine presence will assert itself wherever there are people with ears to hear. The River is flowing, and we may drink or get swept off our feet. If we are lucky, we get to do both.

Intelligence is the ability to consider
a proposition without accepting it.

—Aristotle

• PART ONE •

What Religions Tell Us About God

The God That Stands By

Often, when we in the West encounter Eastern religions, we are put off by the idea of the "impersonal" God. We have a bias in favor of a personal, loving God who is interested in us on an individual basis.

There is nothing wrong with this bias, in itself; the personal God is important to us because it is the God of our experience. Our mythology speaks to us of a God that repeatedly intervenes on the believer's behalf. This is the God that made Sarah fertile beyond her years; who led the Israelites across the Sea of Reeds on dry ground; the God that raised Jairus's daughter from the dead. This God affords us full attention when we request an audience, and is deeply concerned with even the pettiest details of our daily lives.

What, then, do we make of the God who allows six million of "his" people to be tortured and murdered; who allows thousands to die in earthquakes and other natural disasters; who allows children to die by the tens-of-thousands of famine and disease around the world, and suffers the infant to be born only to die of AIDS soon after? What of the God that does *not* intervene? What of the God that stands by, hands-off, unmoved by such suffering and tragedy?

What the religions of the West fail to do is to see God in his or her entirety. Entirety, like infinity, is difficult for us. It is much more comforting to seek relationship with One who is not ambivalent to our concerns than it is to wrestle with the jackal who will not be pinned down. We want a deity who attends to us particularly, not a God who is equally concerned with the other five billion human beings on this planet, let alone the whole of the Universe. We want the kind of special treatment that only the personal God can deliver.

But God cannot but be equally interested (or as they say in the East, disinterested) in the whole of Creation, in that the Holy Spirit enjoys union with all. I am by no means saying that the concept of the personal God is erroneous, only that it is incomplete. God is not exclusively personal, nor is God exclusively impersonal. We must move beyond this "either/or" dichotomy if we are to approach God in his or her entirety.

It may help us to know more about the impersonal God as our Eastern brethren see it. For the Taoist who practices the native religion of China, God—the Tao—is an eternal principle, neither loving nor hating, exhorting nor condemning. The Tao gives birth to all things and unto it all things return. "It is the Mother of the Universe," says Lao Tzu, author of the primary Taoist scripture, the *Tao Te Ching,* and yet "it does not choose sides." Through looking at Nature, the Tao is self-evident. There is an order to the Universe in the midst of seeming chaos; there is unity in diversity. With the Tao one always knows where one stands. The Taoist knows where he comes from and where he is going. With the Tao the human being knows herself to be a part of Nature, and does not attempt to wrestle it into submission. The Taoist sees God in the same way nature does. "Look at the lilies of the field and the birds of the air," says Jesus, "they do not sow, nor do they reap, and yet the Creator feeds them." For the Taoist, the perspective of the sparrow or the trout or the wind is the perspective of the human as well. Humankind occupies no exalted position or special dispensation. She is part of the cosmic community. This is indeed an impersonal deity, yet it is by no means a deity who is aloof, separate from its Creation, but instead permeates all. Even

though the Taoist doesn't expect the Tao to intercede in her interest, she perceives a general sense of "rightness" or goodness in the
world as it is and of which she is a part. Far from expecting the
deity to "make everything all right," the Taoist sees her life and
fate (whatever that is) as an integral part of the "rightness" of the
Universe. And this is the gift that Taoism (and other faith traditions that espouse an impersonal deity) bring to us: a perception
of the Universe as community.

The Taoist sages have provided us a model in the familiar symbol for the Tao: two "tadpoles," to use Jeremy Taylor's description, one black, one white, which, in chasing each other's tails,
form a perfect circle, a unity. Neither black nor white, but both.
Not two separate things, but one. Not male or female, but male
and female; neither warm nor cool, but warm *and* cool.

This model of the Tao is particularly useful for us in the West
when approaching the nature of Divinity. Even within our
Western tradition Meister Eckhart acknowledged this paradox
and designated the impersonal aspect of God as "the Godhead."
"God accomplishes," he writes, "but the Godhead does not do
so." This perspective helps make sense of a God who is neither
exclusively personal nor impersonal, but inclusive of both.

We are privileged beings indeed who are invited to enter into
relationship with a personal God who intervenes incessantly on
our behalf, while also being sustained by the God who provides
our ground of being and embraces all the Universe as one, this
God that stands by.

God the Heretic

Heresy. Just the mention of the word conjures up nightmare images of medieval witchhunts and torture at the hands of the Holy Inquisition. "Thank God," we say when we succeed at banishing these thoughts, "that's all in the past." Physical torture and murder may be more infrequent now than in the past, but as long as there are fundamentalists and progressives in any tradition, there will probably be so-called "heretics." The very word sounds diabolical, but in fact, many of history's heretics are now our heroes of faith: Jesus, Buddha, Martin Luther, Baha'u'llah (founder of the Baha'i faith), and many others.

As upsetting as it may be to the more conservative people of faith, God is not concerned with other people's notions of what She can or cannot do, nor where the Spirit can or cannot lead those who listen to Her. In this way, God can be said to be the wild card of the universe. "The Spirit goes where it wills," says Jesus to the Pharisee Nicodemus, "you hear the sound of it, but you do not know where it comes from, or where it is going."

In his time, Jesus was the fundamentalist's worst nightmare. Here was a man who habitually made disturbing statements that often hinted at his being God. Blasphemy! Yet, as Christians

13

believe, God chose to become human. If that was heresy to the Jewish fundamentalists in his day, very well. God is a heretic. I doubt God loses much sleep over this.

Nowadays, with the archetype of the Goddess arising in the collective consciousness of the people of this planet, the Christian fundamentalists are up in arms about the Goddess "heresy" invading the church. I think we would be wise to remember the mistakes of our past, and to be open to the wind of the Spirit, especially when She ventures into unlikely places. If God wishes to be known as the Goddess for a while, why should that upset me? Instead, I should be listening closely, because I wouldn't want to miss anything! If the Goddess is heresy to the Christian fundamentalists, very well. Again, God is a heretic, a fool, a trickster, a joker, a wild card. God does not need the permission of Jerry Falwell or the Traditional Values Coalition to do God's work in the world—or God's play!

Paul warned that what God does is *skandalon*—a scandal, a stumbling block. When one truly endeavors to follow the Spirit, scandal comes with the territory. The fundamentalist is not evil, just insecure. The enormity of God is overwhelming, so God is made into a manageable image. This is fine. The trouble comes when the religious fundamentalist says "my manageable image is the real God, and no other," and tries to silence anyone who disagrees. This is idolatry, since God is way too big to fit into any image manageable by human cognitive capacity.

For instance, it is unthinkable to some Christians that there could be anything to the Hindu belief about Krishna or the other Hindu avatars. An avatar is God when S/he assumes a human body. "When evil stalks the land," Krishna says in the *Bhagavad Gita*, "I take myself a body and put things right." Hindus believe that this has happened many times, and when they consider Jesus of Nazareth as a manifestation of God, they are inclined to believe it. Fundamentalist Christians, however, rarely return the favor, refusing to consider anything but the unique nature of Jesus as anything but the one and only visitation of God. Yet why should it surprise us that an act of love performed once by God (in this case, becoming human) might be done again? Who are we to say what God can or cannot do? Indeed, it seems very likely that if God chose to come to one people, God might also choose to come to another, and that this visit might not duplicate any other, but be a unique expression of the Divine love to each unique culture.

That God would give godself to all peoples seems only natural to me, and, in fact, just like something She would do. It is natural, too, that every peoples' experience of God would be somehow unique, and that their images and expression of faith and worship be unique as well. And, distressing as that may be to those who think they hold a patent on God, this is as it should be. The fundamentalists would have us believe that the True Faith is established by those with the biggest stick, and this is not Jesus' way at all.

Everyone who has followed the Spirit and walked by faith has been called a heretic by the religiously entrenched. We should not be distressed at this, but remember that we are in the company of prophets, saints, martyrs, artists, and sages. For if any people, inspired by the Spirit and their own creativity, image God in their own unique way, it is hard to believe that God has anything but delight for them. Diversity is God's way (just look at the Creation!).

Regardless of our images, God will go right on giving birth, loving, and suffering with us. But God will also go right on taking the people and things we love from us, without explanation or justification. This is the mystery we live with. As Shiva, God dances whatever dance God pleases. It is not our business to keep up with the whims of the Divine. We know what we are to do. Mechtild tells us plainly: "Live welcoming to all."

The Sacrificed God

From infancy I have heard and believed the Gospel of Christ, and yet never have I understood the crucifixion. This did not occur to me as a child; it was just another of those inexplicable equations that parents gave and kids accepted. After my invaluable years as the prodigal son, however, I returned to the faith of my family. But this time, I did not accept the pat answers nor play the power-games. When something didn't make sense to me, I stalked it until I pinned it down. When I came to the vicarious atonement on the cross I met my match. I scrambled through innumerable commentaries and systematic theologies (an oxymoron, I think) trying to find a suitable explanation. Just what happened up there on that cross, anyway? "Jesus died for my sins" makes no sense in itself. How does an historical event 2000 years removed have the slightest bearing upon my life today? What are the cosmic mechanics involved? What exactly happened on the metaphysical level? I found a lot of words, but no answers. Not only that, how could I reconcile the God of wrath my Calvinism taught with the loving Father of Jesus' teachings?

Then I ran across a Catholic theologian who used the phrase "the mystery of redemption." That's it! Of course! There is no human explanation: it is a mystery. That I could take on faith. I

16

didn't need to understand it—it was beyond human comprehension.

That answer satisfied me for many years, until I began to study a little farther afield. When I picked up the *Upanishads*, the later collection of Hindu scripture, I read about Prajapati, the primeval being alone in the void. Prajapati was all that was at the time, and when he thought the words "I wish I had a body," lo, he had one. But he desired not to be alone even more than he desired a body, and so he performed the first sacrifice. He offered up his own body to be the stuff of the universe. This Hindu Creation myth casts Prajapati in the peculiar role of being the sacrificer, the sacrifice, and the god to whom the sacrifice is offered. This Prajapati posed many questions about my Christology—is this a myth revealing the work of the Pre-incarnate Word? In the beginning of John's gospel it is written "through him all things were made." But the word rendered "were made" is *egeneto*, which is more correctly rendered "became." If through the Word all things became, we get a picture through Prajapati of the universe as the body of God, offered up for his/her own pleasure, the pleasure of community with his/her Creations. It foreshadows the Crucifixion, and as we shall see, forms the beginning of a cosmic continuity of which the Cross is the paramount sign. Even in the celebration of the Eucharist, we echo Prajapati's act: Christ is the sacrificer, the sacrifice, and the God to whom the sacrifice is offered.

One way of understanding Christ is as the unique product of the union of matter and the Spirit of God. Prajapati, then, is the Eastern equivalent of the Cosmic Christ, in whom "we live and move and have our being" throughout all eternity. This is panentheism, the union of the Spirit of God with the material universe. What does this have to do with the gory tragedy of the Crucifixion? Simply that in the Cross we are given an unquestionable symbol of reality: that the spirit of God remains in union with flesh, even though we taunt, spit on him/her and torture him/her, even though we murder him/her. On the cross, Jesus gave us a powerful symbol of what has always been true: despite our ghastly offenses, God remains enfleshed among us. As Alan Watts states in his excellent book *Behold the Spirit*: "God has wedded himself to humanity, has united his divine essence with our inmost being 'for better for worse, for richer for poorer, in sickness and in health' for all eternity.... The fact is the fact: we have been given union with God whether we like it or not, want it or not, know it or not."

The crucifixion was not for the satisfaction of a bloodthirsty Deity who must have an object upon which to unleash his vengeance, but the result of a loving God who does not strike back or interfere, letting our own resentment and violence run its course, which resulted, as it so often does, in murder. As Raymond Schwager, S.J. writes in *Must There Be Scapegoats?*, "Jesus could die for all because all had already turned against him. All joined together against him and by crucifying him, concretely transferred to him their resentment against God and their will to kill." "For the love that creates the world," writes Ian Davie, "is the love that lets it be, and the love that lets it be is the love that suffers its being so."

The redemption may not end with us, either. Perhaps God, too, needs to be redeemed. In Jung's *Answer to Job*, God's permitting of Job's suffering is unethical, and the immaturity of the Old Testament Yahweh is not redeemed until he/she, in Christ, endures like suffering. Indeed, in Davie's *Jesus Parusha*, he says "Jesus consents to die in order that our humanity shall no longer be separated from his. In the cry of dereliction from the Cross ['Why have you forsaken me'], he experiences abandonment by God.... In his own death, he suffers the death of all." Not until death did Jesus experience the totality of the human experience. And then, God could be reconciled with us.

In Prajapati, we see the divinity of our being. In the crucifixion, we see the humanity of God's. And yet they are mirrors of the same reality. To quote Davie again, "Must we not say that there is an eternal Passion of Creation enacted in the unfolding drama of the universe, and a temporal Passion of Redemption which is the enactment in time of that eternal Passion; and yet that there are not two Passions, but one?"

Two Eyes, One Object

A Comparison of Dieties as Found in the
Bhagavad-Gita *and the Poetry of Jelaluddin Rumi*

Having endeavored to do the impossible, comparing the unknowable to the manifest, I am somewhat surprised to find more like than unlike. At first pondering, the deities as described in the Hindu *Gita* and Rumi's prolific poems and letters are as irreconcilable as possible. The God of the most tolerant and inclusive of all the great traditions, Hinduism, capable of embracing any form, provides a sharp contrast to Allah, forbidder of divine forms.

Yet although Rumi's Allah bears scarce resemblance to the often forbidding God of the holy *Koran*, the Islamic "flavor" is retained, even in translation. Rumi's Allah is not spending much of the text casting ne'er-do-wells into everlasting Hellfire, a prevelant image in the *Koran*, but instead plays the sly seductress, dancing around us, wooing us into passionate relations. Krishna, as spoken of in the *Gita*, is also a break with tradition. Whereas the God of the *Upanishads* is cosmic and philosophical, Krishna is the personal God, and like Rumi's Allah, he calls us to intimate relationship.

Flying in the face of the above statement is the paradox that both of these personal gods are essentially unknowable. Krishna tells Arjuna that he is ignorant of his higher existence.... Veiled in the magic of my discipline, I elude most men.... I know all crea-

19

tures that have been, that now exist, and that are yet to be; but Arjuna, no one knows me.[1]

What Krishna probably means here is that no one knows him in his entirety. To truly know Krishna, the supreme Lord, would be beyond the human capacity for comprehension. Whereas the *Gita's* claim is qualified, Islam makes few bones about this "unknowability;" the *Koran* seldom tires of reminding us of our ignorance. Yet in Rumi's vision the Supremely Unknowable, though never fully grasped, is at least approachable. "When you eventually see through the veils to how things really are," he writes, "you will keep saying again and again, 'This is certainly not like we thought it was!'"[2]

Part of the deities' unknowability has to do with their transcendence. Both are, in their own ways, immanent as well, but the imagery of the transcendent is strong in both bodies of work. Krishna knows that we (through Arjuna) are aware of his immanence, and so strives to make us aware that what is tangible, ordinary, and most of all present, is also that which is beyond and ungraspable. "This is my lower nature; know my higher nature too, the life-force that sustains this universe."[3] Krishna's sovereignty extends far beyond the world, in fact. "Neither sun nor moon, nor fire illumines my highest abode—once there, they do not return."[4] The spatial distance of the God's domain is echoed by Rumi when he tells Allah, "Like a bee you fill hundreds of homes with honey, though yours is a long flight from here."[5] Rumi's God does not seem to be at home in this world. He is an ever-present, yet ever-absent visitor.

Humankind, recognizing the spark of divinity in itself, apparently also needs reminding that God is also beyond not only the world, but humankind as well. The danger is of over-identity with the deity—the remedy seems to be putting humans in their place. Arjuna, terrified by the vision of Krishna's entirety, has no arguments about his place in the universe, but the practice of mysticism lends itself to possible abuse. There is no greater sin in Islam that to suggest that Allah could be incarnate, yet the Sufis had this annoying habit of screaming out "I am God!" in the midst of their ecstasies. Rumi says of one man that he cried out, drunk with divinity, "There is no God but me. You should wor-ship me." In the morning, when he was informed of his behavior, he swore, "If I say that again, bring your knives and plunge them into me. God is beyond the body, and I am in this body. Kill me when I say that."[6] The truth lies between the man's two state-ments. Though he cannot deny the experience of divine union, he cannot (on pain of death, most likely) but insist on God's supreme transcendence. Rumi speaks of Allah as being "...in each of my atoms. Each of my raw nerves...."[7] Allah says, "I am so close to you I am distant. I am so mingled with you I am apart. I am so open I am hidden. I am so strong I totter."[8]

Hand in hand with transcendence is omniscience. Krishna speaks plainly of his own numerous incarnations: "I know them all, but you do not, Arjuna."[9] He also says that he is the source of all knowledge, the object to be known and the knower of its final truth.[10] Likewise, Rumi admits humbly "I can't know, only you can."[11] He grapples with profundity, saying,

> You can't be spoken, though you listen to all sound. You can't be written, but you read everything. You don't sleep, yet you're the source of dream-vision. Your ship glides over nothing, deep silence, praise for the ONE, who told Moses on Sinai, You Shall Not See Me.[12]

In the Gita, Krishna spends nearly the entire tenth chapter describing himself and his attributes. He is not just a general, he is the god of war! He is not a sacred month, but the most sacred month; he is not just a poet, he is Vyasa, the greatest poet; he is not happy to be merely an elephant, he is the king's mount; he is not just a weapon, he is a thunderbolt.[13] Krishna is the archetype for all earthly types, like the Vedic Perusha, the archetypal man. Krishna is thus the model, the Platonic ideal, which lends its identity to incarnate forms. Similarly, for Rumi,

> Every object and being in the universe is a jar overfilled with wisdom and beauty, a drop of the Tigris that cannot be contained by any skin. Every jarful spills and makes the earth more shining, as though covered in satin. If the man had seen even a tributary of the great river, he wouldn't have brought the innocence of his gift.[14]

It is in the forms that we catch a glimpse of the ideal. It is through the god of war that we can begin to grasp the excellence of such a general. It is through a stranger's kindness that we can begin to fathom grace. "All giving comes from There, no matter who you think you put your open hand out toward, it's That which gives."[15] It is by this way of knowing that we catch wind of our own divine identity. Rumi says,

> You'll tell it to yourself. Not I, or some other "I," You who are ME!
> As when you fall asleep and go from the presence of your self to the Presence of your Self. You hear That One and you think, "Someone must have communicated telepathically in my sleep."
> You are not a single You, good Friend, you are a Sky and an Ocean, a tremendous YHUUUUUU, a nine hundred times huge drowning place for all your hundreds of you's.[16]

The deity, then is more complicated than simply immanence and transcendence; he is so closely interwoven into our very perception of our surroundings and ourselves as to be completely inseparable. Forgetting such lofty concepts as archetypes, transcendence and omniscience for a moment, one can't even go for a pack of filter Kings without somehow conceptually dealing with God.

> You are my face. No wonder I can't see You. You are the intricate workings of my mind....[17] You are the moon: I am your face in a pool. How could I forget that night you said, holding my head, 'I am yours always. Your love came from me; I am your soul.'"[18]

One doesn't normally think of Islam as being pantheistic, yet Rumi echoes many of Krishna's teachings about the unity of All. Krishna instructs Arjuna, "See all the universe, animate and inanimate, and whatever else you wish to see; all stands here as one in my body."[19] Rumi could very well have been answering the blue-skinned God by saying, "One look at you, and I look at you in all things, looking back at me; those eyes in which all things live and burn."[20] Krishna reveals that, "He who sees me everywhere and sees everything in me will not be lost to me, and I will not be lost to him."[21] This is a grand truth that Rumi learned well, for he instructs his own pupils, saying, "Let your eyes see God everywhere. Give up fears and expectations. The Friend, the Beloved, your Soul, is a River with the trees and buds of the world reflected in it."[22] This pantheistic vision holds vast implications, expounded on by all mystical traditions. In particular, it is most common to find that once the mystic has accepted himself as a part of the All, he begins to see the All as himself. Rumi says,

> Remember that no man is without it. If man was without it, he would never have said "I," because it is this enemy within him which is saying "I." The day this enemy is found and erased, or shed and crucified, that day the real "I" is found. But this "I" is a different "I." This "I" means you and I and everybody; it is an all "I."[22]

Rumi implies in the above verse the painful dying process inherent in spiritual growth, and the resulting wisdom one is able to grasp as a result. Though Krishna makes no mention of this important catharsis, he acknowledges the importance of this enlightenment by saying, "When he perceives the unity existing in separate creatures and how they expand from unity, he attains the infinite spirit."[23]

This is, for Rumi, a dangerous position to take, considering the consequences of blasphemy in medieval Islamic culture. Hats (and turbans) off to those Sufi theologians who turned all kinds of philosophic gymnastics trying to reconcile the orthodox Allah with the divinity of their experience. Of the orthodox, Rumi wrote "...be calm with those in duality."[24] One must wonder if they were so patient with him.

Not satisfied to inform Arjuna that he is in all things, Krishna continues to say that he is all things, past, present, and future. When he says "I am the rite, the sacrifice, the libation for the dead, the healing herb, the sacred hymn, the clarified butter, the fire, the oblation,"[25] he is, from a Vedic point of view, laying out an equation: The Sacrifice = the Universe. Therefore, if Krishna = the Sacrifice, then Krishna = the Universe. And he claims this status for all of time: "I am the self abiding in the heart of all creatures; I am their beginning, their middle, and their end."[26] This, too, finds its parallel in Rumi, when he relates simply to his friends, "It's the Voice that first said, 'There is no Reality but God.'

There is only God."[27] Husam pulls him by his ear and shouts at him to wash his mouth, but the damage is done, the truth is out. Rumi even announces the Persian equivalent of *"Tat tvam asi,"* "You are that."[28] Krishna claims to be all things to all men, saying,

"I am the way, sustainer, lord, witness, shelter, refuge, friend, source, dissolution, stability, treasure, and unchanging seed. I am heat that withholds and sends down the rains; I am immortality and death; both being and nonbeing am I."[29]

Again, Rumi must experience this from the other side, grasping intuitively what Krishna knows so well: "Thirsty and dry, I complain, but everything is made of water! Lonely, yet my head leans against your shirt! My wounded hands, your hands."[30]

Once having accepted the Unity of All in God, it is not long before we consider the Unity of Gods in All. Ecumenism has always been a touchy subject in exclusivistic traditions, especially Christianity and Islam, but also, apparently in many Hindu sects as well. Krishna does not pussy-foot around the subject, but states bluntly "When devoted men sacrifice to other deities with faith, they sacrifice to me, Arjuna, however aberrant the rites.[31] Knowing me as the enjoyer of sacrifices and penances, lord of all worlds, and friend of all creatures, he finds peace."[32] Rumi comforts his listeners with a teaching story about four men who speak different languages (and so can't understand each other) all asking for a bit of money. A ruckus soon erupts, and Rumi ends the tale, saying,

If a many-languaged master had been there, he could have made peace and told them: I can give each of you what you want with this one coin. Trust me, keep quiet, and you four enemies will agree. I know a silent, inner meaning that makes of your four words one wine."[33]

Speaking more directly, he says,

We can't help being thirsty, moving toward the voice of water. Milk-drinkers draw close to the mother. Muslims, Christians, Jews, Buddhists, Hindus, shamans, everyone hears the intelligent sound and moves, with thirst, to meet it.[34]

Another important point of convergence is with regard to the believer, the beloved of God. One of the primary topics of importance in the *Gita* is action. Krishna makes it very clear that his devoted should not renounce action itself, but the fruit of action. This is demonstrated by the deity when he tells Arjuna, "The lord of the world does not create agency or actions, or a union of fruits with actions; but his being unfolds into existence."[35] Krishna strives for no object of desire, yet still he must act, for "What if I did not engage relentlessly in action? ...These worlds would collapse if I did not perform action."[36] Rumi calls the fruit of actions by another name: "Don't let others lead you," he says, "They may be blind, or worse, vultures. Reach for the rope of God. And what is that? Putting aside self-will."[37] Self-will, wanting for the self, desiring the fruit of action.... Krishna commands us, saying, "Surrender all actions to me, and fix your reason on your inner self; without hope or possessiveness, your fever subdued, fight the battle!"[38] We are told by Rumi that one who can follow this example is himself divine: "The One who acts without regard to getting anything back is God. Or a Friend of God."[39]

Friendship with God is the sole domain of the personal diety—being indifferent to God is not nearly so comforting or appealing—and it is in this area that both deities excel. "Keep your mind on me," Krishna tells Arjuna, "be my devotee, sacrificing, bow to me—you will come to me, I promise, for you are dear to me."[40] If the Blue One seems to be a little chilly, Allah more than compensates in his gushing: "Noah, Noah," said God, "I will raise Canaan and all these others from the dead if you wish. I don't want you to grieve."[41] This demonstrates not merely fondness from the deity (Krishna could just as well be talking to his bloodhound), but that the human is respected by the deity, to the point that the thought of the beloved in emotional pain causes like pain in the Divine. When Muhammed has been so overwhelmed by a vision that he passes out, Gabriel cradles him in his arms. "Awe serves for strangers," Rumi comments, but "this close-hugging love is for friends."[42]

It would be an understatement to say that this study has been revealing for me. Hinduism and Islam seem the most diametrically opposed religions the planet knows, and yet it is telling that in the mystical literature of each, we find a unified vision of the cosmos. Each retains the flavor of the original, yet Huxley's "perennial philosophy" runs like a thread through each. Rumi even concedes (amazing!) to reincarnation: "I burn away; laugh; my ashes are alive! I die a thousand times: My ashes dance back—A thousand new faces."[43] And this is perpetually our experience: the journey inward is familiar, it is only the outer paths by which we have come together that open onto different plains. The single object of divinity, seen through different eyes, must of course be understood in the context of the seekers' prior disparate experience; the inner experience of the mystics, we find, agrees in most every detail.

NOTES

1   Vyasa; Barbara Stoler Miller, trans. *The Bhagavad-Gita: Krishna's Counsel in Time of War.* (New York: Bantam Books, 1986), p. 74.

2   Rumi, Jelaluddin; Coleman Barks and John Moyne, trans. *This Longing* (Putney: Threshhold Books, 1988), p. 22.

3   *Gita*, p. 74.

4   *Ibid.*, p. 128.

5   Rumi, Jelaluddin; Coleman Barks, trans. *We Are Three* (Athens: Maypop Books, 1987), p. 22.

6   Rumi, Jelaluddin; Coleman Barks, trans. *Delicious Laughter* (Athens: Maypop Books, 1990), p. 30.

7   Rumi, Jelaluddin; Andrew Harvey, trans. *Love's Fire* (Ithaca: Meeramma Publications, 1988), p. 68.

8   *Ibid.*, p. 24.

9   *Gita*, p. 49.

10   *Ibid.*, p. 130.

11   *Love's Fire*, p. 28.

12   *We Are Three*, p. 9.

13 *Gita*, p. 93-94.

14 *We Are Three*, p. 46.

15 *Delicious Laughter*, p. 50.

16 *This Longing,* p. 49.

17 *Ibid.*, p. 58.

18 *Love's Fire*, p. 53.

19 *Gita*, p. 98.

20 *Love's Fire*, p. 22.

21 *Gita*, p. 67.

22 *This Longing*, p. xv.

23 *Gita*, p. 119.

24 *This Longing*, p. 60.

25 *Gita*, p. 85.

26 *Ibid.*, p. 92.

27 *Delicious Laughter*, p. 126.

28 *We Are Three*, p. 40.

29 *Gita*, p. 86.

30 *We Are Three*, p. 3.

31 *Ibid.*, p. 11.

32 *Ibid.*, p. 25.

33 *Gita*, p. 59.

34 *Ibid.*, p. 44.

35 *Ibid.*, p. 44.

36 *We Are Three*, p. 44.

37 *Gita*, p. 45.

38 *This Longing*, p. 26.

39 *Gita*, p. 152.

40   *This Longing*, p. 52.

41   *Delicious Laughter*, p. 106.

42   *This Longing*, p. 96.

As Above, So Below

Politics and religion: eternal and inseparable twins that have wrecked unrivaled havoc with our history. They are, it seems, joined at the hip, and just as we strenuously forbid their fraternizing in the courts, so too shall they be prohibited in tandem at Thanksgiving Day Dinner.

Separation of church and state is a noble aspiration; yet none of us, I fear, separate the two in our own personal paradigms. This was much more obvious in times past. For a score of centuries, the government had been a divinely ordained hierarchy, with the King at the top, his ministers beneath him, the nobles beneath them, followed by the merchants, with the peasants at the bottom. It was divinely ordained because this was not only the governmental paradigm, but the paradigm of the universe as well.

Therefore God, in both the Hebrew and Christian traditions, is the King of the Universe, beneath whom are the angels, and finally, lowly and wretched humankind. Our scriptures are based on this model, and it is impossible to read the Psalms for very long before we are confronted with it.

As a young fundamentalist, this bothered me not at all. Indeed, my church operated in the same paradigm, with the pastor at the

29

head, confident and godly right, not to be questioned by his infe-
riors, and deserving of their love and loyalty. Beneath him were
the deacons (which in the Baptist church are laymen, the equivalent of elders), followed by the men of the congregation, all resting upon the tired backs of the laywomen and children.

Scripturally, it was, as I saw it, "holy" appropriate. In my conversion to Catholicism in the Episcopal Church, I was confirmed
into a similar structure, headed by the Archbishop of Canterbury,
under whom are the presiding bishops of the various member
churches of the Anglican Communion, under which are the
regional bishops, followed by the priests, etc. This medieval
structure might have been appropriate at one time: it was, in fact,
considered by one and all to be the divine blueprint of the universe.

It also gave license to those in power to behave in a manner
similar to God's own behavior in scripture. Therefore, since
Yaweh can be, as scripture shows, bloodthirsty, wrathful, and
punitive, "his" viceroys on Earth were obligated to emulate these
traits.

This has not always been so. Pre-patriarchal society had a very
different sort of structure. Archeological data seems to indicate
that it may have been for the most part egalitarian. As Riane Eisler
points out in her ground-breaking classic, *The Chalice and the
Blade*, European Neolithic society emphasized linking, rather
than ranking, "a partnership society in which neither half of
humanity is ranked over the other and diversity is not equated
with inferiority or superiority." The "partnership" model of society is based upon the principles of community and equality rather
than dominance. Again, society was mirrored in the conception
of divinity. As Nicolas Platon writes in his book *Crete*, "The whole
of life was pervaded by an ardent faith in the goddess Nature, the
source of all Creation and harmony." Neolithic art reveals much
about the society; to quote Eisler again, "Mythical art reflects not
only peoples' attitudes but also their particular form of culture
and social organization. Here the supreme power governing the
universe is a divine Mother who gives her people life, provides
them with material and spiritual nurturance, and who even in

death can be counted on to take her children back into her cosmic womb."

In the pre-patriarchal world, all things were recognized as being connected, parts of a greater whole, which was symbolized in their cosmology as the great and nurturing Goddess.

We no longer live in Neolithic times, nor do we remember them well. We do, however, know the conquering patriarchy only too well. But we are undergoing a paradigm shift on this planet that cannot be ignored. We no longer live in a monarchy, and when I read the Psalms, the portrait received feels odd and wrong. I no longer believe in a monarchy, nor in a "Jacob's Ladder" model of government, as was the norm in medieval times. Furthermore, I witness my friends suffering at the hands of a religious monarchy which is desperately trying to cling to what is an archaic and destructive paradigm.

At the end of the twentieth century we hold an ideal of democracy, where everyone has a voice, and a government of, by, and for the people. But as our political paradigm has evolved, our cosmology and theology must follow suit. With the advent of Liberation theology, we conceive of the church as the body of the faithful, not the vehicle of the hierarchs. With our rediscovery of Creation Spirituality and Native peoples' forms of worship, we see ourselves not as emperors lording over the Earth and her creatures, but as one with her and every manner of being she has birthed. With the dawn of Process Theology we see ourselves as partners with God in the unfolding of the Universe, as integral and necessary companions without whom God could not continue. As the consciousness of the Earth's people has evolved into a paradigm of equality and justice, so are people of faith the world over being ushered by the Spirit into a spiritual democracy, where every voice is God's voice, every heart is the heart of God, and where God's only hands are our own.

God Belongs to Everyone

L ast month, I made my first sojourn to Jerusalem. It was an experience that was exactly what I had hoped for, but not at all what I expected. I could easily speak for an hour about what surprised me, but for our purposes today, I'll only tell you about a couple of things.

Wherever you stand in Jerusalem, the crowning jewel of that beautiful city is the Dome of the Rock, one of the most important mosques in Islam. My companion had been there before, as had several friends, and everyone insisted it was a must-see attraction. So of course it was on our list of things to do. But we soon discovered it would not be so easy. There are about five entrances to the courtyard in which the mosque stands, but the armed guards stationed at those entrances would not let us pass. They told us there was only one entrance we could use, and it was on the other side of the city, by the Wailing Wall.

So we went to the Wailing Wall and passed through the equivalent of airport security. We finally found ourselves in the courtyard alongside a gaggle of other tourists. The dome of the mosque shone gold in the sun, and we marveled at the calligraphy that covers nearly every inch of the exterior of the building. But we were disappointed when we got to the door. They would not let us enter the building, they told us in halting, broken English, because we were not Muslims.

I was crushed. I wish I had known one phrase in Arabic, because I would have dropped to my knees and declared, "There is no God but God, and Mohammad is his prophet!" The willingness to utter this one sentence is, as I understand it, the only requirement for becoming a Muslim, and I would have done it if I had known it in their sacred tongue.

But I'm pretty sure that for that gatekeeper, "Muslim" was pretty much synonymous with "Palestinian," and the puffy white Irish-looking guy with the Franciscan tonsure was not going to be fooling anybody.

It made me sad. The Dome of the Rock is one of the glories of Islam—it speaks to the whole world of Islam's beauty, power, and transcendence. It calls to all people, saying, "Come, taste, and see that Allah is good!" I so wanted to see that mosque, because I happen to know that Allah is pretty tasty.

It reminded me of the scene in the lost Gospel of Thomas where the religious authorities are refusing to minister to those people they do not consider worthy of their instruction. And Jesus, who, as we all know, can really get his righteous indignation on when he wants to, says, "Damn you, Pharisees! You are like dogs guarding the water trough! You neither drink nor allow anyone else to do so!"

This is not just a Muslim phenomenon, of course. Nor is it a Jewish one. Or a Christian one. Any faith that has regarded itself as the One True Way has defined itself as much by who was left out as by who was allowed in. And the unfortunate truth is that, at one time or another, this has been true of most faiths.

This is what makes the Chaplaincy Institute and the Interfaith movement we are so proud to be a part of so special, so vital, so important. Our students are standing up in the marketplace, they are going against the grain, they are bearing witness to a world that defines itself by those who have and those who have not, those who are in and those who are out, and are prophetically proclaiming that one divine, sublime truth that all religions know but have such a hard time embracing: there are no outsiders. There is no "them," and there is no "us."

For many people it is uncomfortable to hear that there is no religion that has a monopoly on truth, or wisdom, or salvation. Discomfort is a good thing. Our graduates are not looking to be popular, they are looking to bring the light of faith and the balm of peace both to those who believe they deserve it, and those who have always been excluded, and to do it without distinction.

In this way they are a witness to the world, to our leaders, and to the religious authorities: that divinity is the birthright of all peoples, regardless of religion, or race, or economic status, or gender or sexual orientation, or mental health, or physical health, or even criminal record. We are calling off the dogs, and inviting everyone to take a drink. Because Allah is good, Adonai is tasty, Brigit is delicious, Jesus is sweet, Shiva is sublime, Buddha is the bomb, and Zarathustra is *muy gusta*.

One other thing that surprised me on our trip. The Church of the Holy Sepulchre is the most holy shrine in all of Christendom. Over here is the spot where Jesus was crucified. Over there the place where he was laid in the tomb. But this church is shared by four different Christian denominations, each of which claim one corner for themselves, distrust all of the others, and watch each other like hawks for the smallest infraction upon their "turf." But none of them hold the key to the building. The key is held by a Muslim family, a neutral party, whose responsibility has been, for the last thousand years, to unlock the building in the morning, and secure it again at night.

For me, this is interfaith in a nutshell. As each faith has traditionally guarded the divine as its own special property, the key is held by none of them. The interfaith movement has a special responsibility: to throw open the doors and invite all people in. Our ordinands, in each of their own ministries, are already doing that. Our alumni are doing it everyday in a hundred different places. This school supports and upholds them in what is, after all, the only endeavor that will ever bring this planet peace.

Thank you for being here, families, friends, partners, loved ones. Thank you for supporting them. They can't do it without you. No one can. And it *so* needs to be done. *Namaste*.

• PART TWO •

What Religions Tell Us About Being Human

There is No Salvation (Apart from the Body)

T he body has gotten a bad rap in the West. From the Greek philosophers to modern, conservative, religious theologians, the history of the body in Western thought is grim. A tragic mistranslation renders St. Paul as saying that the body is opposed to the spirit (Gal. 5:17), to the result of two millenia of sincere people mortifying the flesh for "spiritual" purposes. Augustine asserted that "the soul makes war with the body," and Calvin viewed earthly human existence as being no better than a worm. Even St. Francis condescendingly made reference to his own body as "Brother Ass." The magnitude of psychological suffering this has caused in literally millions of people through the ages is criminal. We have been convinced that the physical world, and with it, our physical selves, are corrupt, depraved, and worthy of our scorn and abuse. The body has been viewed as a cruel cage from which the soul longs to escape to some ethereal, nebulous realm.

But to many traditions, this scorn seems strange. In Native traditions, the body is a gift to be loved, cared for, and celebrated. In the East it is the highest earthly privilege to be born in a human body, for only from it can enlightenment be reached. In fact, for many traditions, salvation apart from the body is impossible. In the rituals of the Hawaiian Kahuna tradition, the intellect and the spirit are incommunicado, and the body alone, through ritual, can serve as message-bearer. In Hinduism, Hatha Yoga promises salvation through the discipline of one's body, and in Buddhism it is the close attention to the "environment" of the body that brings *satori*, or "breakthrough" for the Spirit. With this weight of opinion from our sister faiths, perhaps it is not inappropriate to reconsider the body in the Western Christian tradition. Is this violence toward the physical truly borne out in scripture, or has our reading of it been prejudiced by a tradition of negative ecclesiastical opinion?

Our Judaic heritage knows little of this prejudice. The Jews have always viewed the world as a blessing, and with it, their lives. The pre-exilic Jews did not pine for the afterlife and a non-physical existence. For them, to be human was a noble thing; they felt worthy to stand tall before the Creator. The afterlife was infrequently speculated upon in the time that the Scriptures were written. The Jews focused their energy on the reality of this life, trusting God to do the just thing in the next.

For the Christian, the Incarnation itself should say something. Unless we fall back on docetism, the presence of Christ in human form can be nothing less than God's resounding affirmation of the created order. How could God reside in or bother to redeem the vile and irredeemable? We are even promised an eternal incarnate life in a resurrected body, like Christ's, "of flesh and bone."

We should even question the validity of the soul-body dualism. William Blake wrote, "[The human] has no body distinct from the soul, for that called body is a portion of soul discern'd by the five senses, the chief inlets of soul in this age." Meister Eckhart concurs, saying, "The soul loves the body. And consider too how it is that the body is more in the soul than the soul is in the body." St. Thomas Aquinas even tells us that "the soul united with the body is more like God than the soul separated from the body."

We find, when we are willing to search, that the opinion of many throughout the history of Christendom is that it is the body which is the source of our greatest joys and even of our "spiritual" progress. For instance, it is Hildegard's belief that by cultivating the earthly, we create the heavenly. And for Dame Julian of Norwich it is our very sensuality, "grounded in Nature," which "enables us to receive gifts that lead to everlasting life."

A more radical, Biblical approach might be suggested by the immanently troublesome verse from John's gospel, where Jesus says "No one comes to the Father except by me." What are we to make of this? It seems that this is the ultimate tribalistic, exlusivist claim for Christianity, but it need not be so. We only run into trouble if we consider the speaker to be Christ in the historic person of Jesus of Nazareth. But just as Christ Jesus is the result of the union of God's Spirit with a specific human body, so also is the Cosmic Christ the result of the union of God's Spirit with the cosmos, of all physical realty. If we are willing to consider Jesus as speaking in this verse from the perspective of his eternal Incarnation as the ground of all being, we hear a very different message, indeed: salvation apart from the physical, the body, is impossible.

This confirms for us in our own tradition what we have heard from our brothers and sisters in other faith traditions: that the body is a means of spiritual progress and a source of blessing and joy. As Nicholas of Cusa affirms, "Only in a finite fashion is the infinite form received."

More Than Men

I propose that it is more difficult to be a man today than in any previous era. We are unsure of exactly what it is that a man is supposed to be. Our celluloid role models appear to us now as inane caricatures, and we feel more than a little guilt about the sins of our fathers. We are unsure as to what genuine alternatives might be ours. Many of us who are feminists sense within ourselves an atrophied presence, the *anima*, as Jung called it, our feminine nature whom we have, through myriad generations, sought to suppress, and with "her," as Elémere Zolla writes, we have also lost her gifts: "the art of listening to forewarnings, of accepting frailty, of feeling tenderness toward the cosmos. Masculine regimentation, planning, [and] utilitarian exploitation have grown to the extent of bringing us to the verge of self-destruction."

This suspicion about the feminine latent in the man and the masculine latent in the woman is an intuition which has pervaded every culture. Mythologies around the planet have equated the division of the sexes as a great cosmic breach which can only be healed by reunification. In the early Christian Gnostic scriptures it is written that "in the days when Eve was in Adam, death did not exist. When she was separated from him, death came into existence. If he reenters and takes [her] unto himself death will not exist." This split into two distinct "natures" ushered in dualism, which the medieval Catholic mystic John Scotus Eriugena believed to be the original sin. When the feminine was removed from the previously androgynous Adam, the world fell out of harmony and into conflict. Eriugena's remedy is reunification, which he said would result in the reunification of Earth and heaven.

Sages of every tradition have perceived this connection and many have spiritual exercises which facilitate this unity. In Taoism, there is a meditation in which the believer balances the masculine and feminine energies within his or her own body, the union of which produces offspring: the "foetus of immortality." The offspring is one's own soul, complete and whole.

A similar meditation is found in the Tantric branch of Hinduism. In this practice, the male energy is represented by the figure of the *kundalini*, the serpent of the spine, which as the practice progresses will eventually rise, passing through each of the *chakras* or energy centers of the body, ultimately uniting with the "thousand-petalled lotus," the final *chakra* which represents the feminine energy of the universe. This unification destroys the meditator's illusions of duality, and sets him or her free, knowing that, in truth, the cosmos is One. In Tibetan Tantric (Buddhist) practice, one who has pierced this veil of illusion becomes *Jivan Mukta*, for whom, as Franklin Abbot puts it, "opposites do not hold and absolute liberty allows that person to fly, to be in two places at once, to walk on water and produce other assorted miracles."

The union of the gendered energies, therefore, traditionally affords an adept supernatural powers. This is found in places as diverse as the mythologies of Greece (as evidenced by the blind and doubly transsexual prophet Tiresias) and the shamanic practices of Native African and Native American spiritualities. The African priest of the Ndembu tribe is considered both male and female, and homosexuality in Native American practice is, in the Sioux and many other tribes, traditionally indicative of great spiritual sensitivity.

A reason for this is that wholeness is not very far removed from holiness. The person in whom androgyny manifests is more like God, who is not sexless, but sex*ful*, being both Father and Mother of the universe. In Jewish mysticism, God's name, *YHWH*, can be divided symbolically to show that the first *Y* corresponds to the Father, the *H* to the Mother, and *WH* to the cosmic androgene, the Son/Daughter of which we are all a part.

Gnostic Christianity has dealt with these questions extensively, and holds for us the key to the masculine dilemma. Gnostic scripture describes the soul as existing in suffering: "But when she (the soul) weeps and repents, then [God] will have mercy on her and will make her womb turn from outside and will turn it again inward...then the soul becomes again what she was before." Elaine Pagels comments that this "suggests that the soul in everyone, men and women alike, recovers its original androgyny...by withdrawing from mere sensation, and turning inward." For men this means having the courage to become quiet, to listen instead of speaking, to reflect inwardly as well as outwardly. The reclaiming of our feminine natures does not detract, does not make us any *less* men, but in fact it makes us *more* than men. Women, through the women's liberation movement, have rediscovered and reclaimed their *animus*, their masculinity, proving themselves to be equal to the male, and because they have masculinity in addition to their femininity, they are more than women. Until men are reunited with their feminine selves, women will continue to surpass them spiritually.

These observations are not lost on our Western Christian tradition, either. Matthew Fox, in a comparison of the images of the soul in the writings of medieval Christian mystics Meister Eckhart and Teresa of Avila, notes that "to be authentically human means that the male is in touch with the deep female within himself," and points out the preponderance of feminine images of the soul in Eckhart (a man) and the many masculine images of the soul in Teresa (a women). He also reminds us of Jung's warning that "one way to lose one's soul is for the male to seek the feminine wholly outside himself and for the female to seek the masculine exclusively outside herself."

Jesus, in the Gospel of Thomas, promises us, "When you make the inner as the outer, the outer as the inner, and the upper as the lower, and when you make the male and female into one, so the male shall not be male and the female shall not be female, then shall you enter paradise."

Morality and Work

While a student at the conservative evangelical college where I spent my undergraduate years, I was invited to the wedding of a classmate. I didn't know her fiancé well at all save for a couple of coffee shop conversations we happened to fall into, but he seemed an amiable sort. I knew that he worked with some other of my acquaintances from college, and a point was made of this during the wedding when the groom and all of the groomsmen donned dark sunglasses and their security passes from the factory where they built missiles and other weapons for the military.

Their humor was not lost on me—I like to think I'm sillier than the next guy—but the four of them, upstanding young Christian men with spotless reputations, publicly admitting that they work where they do.... I was uncomfortably distracted by this incongruity. Perhaps they had never given a second thought to the use to which their labor may someday be applied. Not only did it not seem to bother them, but it didn't seem to occur to anyone at the college as odd, either. I was used to playing the Lone Liberal at my school, but it forced me to think about what is and what is not appropriate work for a Christian. When the bombs fell on Iraq, did they wonder if this murder was the work of their own hands? I wonder. It echoes the irony in *The Last Temptation of Christ* where Jesus is under contract by the Romans to produce crucifixion crosses. I racked my brain for some reference in the Gospels to making an appropriate living. This bothers me a little, in that I can't think of any explicit word on the subject.

For our Buddhist brethren, the primary practice of faith is guided by the Noble Eightfold path, which includes Right Understanding, Right Thought, Right Speech, Right Action, Right Effort, Right Mindfulness, Right Concentration, and Right Livelihood. It is this last that I am concerned with here. According to Buddhist scripture, Right Livelihood forbids the disciple to earn a living that is contrary to the spirit of Right Speech and Right Action: "Monks, these five trades ought not to be followed by a lay follower. Which five? Trade in weapons, trade in living beings, trade in meat, trade in liquor, and trade in poison" (*Anguttaranikaya* 5, 177 III). Elsewhere, scripture specifies butchers, fowlers, trappers, hunters, fishers, robbers, executioners, and jailors (*Majjhimanikaya* 51 I).

Why is it that Christianity has nothing to say on this subject? Why is it that none of the above listed occupations are considered inconsistent with the Christian life in our culture?

The Gospels may be silent about occupation explicitly, but we can certainly infer some things from Jesus' actions. Two instances come to mind: the story of the dishonest tax-collector, Zaccheus, and the woman caught in adultery. In the former, Zaccheus was a man of diminutive stature who climbed a tree in order to see Jesus as he passed through the city. Jesus, to everyone's surprise, called Zaccheus down and informed him that he would join him for a meal. During the course of the meal, Jesus' presence worked a transformation within Zaccheus, a conversion. He admitted his wrongdoing in extracting more taxes from the populace than they owed. Zaccheus was eager to make amends and to start a new sort of life. Jesus didn't insist that he give up tax collecting, just that he be fair.

In the other story, Jesus rescued a woman from an angry mob set on stoning her to death, the appropriate Mosaic punishment for adultery. Jesus didn't lecture her about morality or the Law.

She knew those things, and she knew her occupation was forbidden. Jesus didn't coerce her into repentance, his mere presence was enough to transform her. "Go and sin no more." Jesus said, and no more. Tradition tells us that this woman turned out to be Mary Magdalene, the first to behold the risen Christ.

A Buddhist story tells of a notorious murderer who terrorized the kingdom. The inevitable happened. When the murderer confronted the Buddha, intending no good, the very presence of the holy man shook him to his very core. He dropped his weapons and knelt before the Buddha declaring that he wanted to become a monk. The Buddha embraced him and ordained him. In each of these stories, authentic encounters with the Holy One result in a personal transformation that includes the convert's means of living. The implicit message is clear: encounter with the Holy redeems and transforms the whole of life.

The Gospels do have more to say about our occupations. When Jesus was called to task for picking grain to eat on the Sabbath, and for healing on the Sabbath, he made it clear that helping, healing, and providing for others is always more important than any explicit Law, even if that Law is from Yahweh's own hands (as in the Ten Commandments). In the story of Jesus' visit with his friends Mary and Martha, it is made clear that adoration—quality time with loved ones, with Nature or with the silent presence of the Divine—is of far greater import than having all the dishes clean, or having the closets in order.

I am still disturbed when I recall my friends' wedding. Not so much that these are friends who are making painful choices in hard times, weighing the moral implications of their employment over the hunger of their families, etc., but because they are completely unconscious of the incongruity between their work and their faith. It has challenged me to examine my own life for such oversights, in the light of a spiritual tradition that calls for daily conversion and continuous revelation.

An End to Suffering

We crave: a two-word analysis of the human condition. In the United States, it is a drive responsible for our criminal consumerism, for our need to "keep up with the Joneses" even if the Joneses are plummeting lemmings. We are not satisfied, nor can we quite figure out exactly what it is we lack that produces this ache of dissatisfaction. The American way of life has degenerated into a crisis of addiction, with most of us trying to fill the void within us with whatever promises to take away the angst of existence, however temporarily. We crave something beyond our experience, and the pain of that longing haunts us in every lonely moment, every empty victory, every success or acquisition that disappoints us when the smoke of novelty clears and we find ourselves alone again with our dissatisfaction. The great Buddhist scripture, the *Dhammapada*, tells us that "from craving arises sorrow and from craving arises fear."

What can we do? It is not an easy problem to solve. When we try to numb our pain chemically, we become addicted to the chemical, which will eventually kill us. When we try to smother it in the security of others' love, we smother the love of our friends. For many in our culture, the Twelve Step process has been their salvation in regard to their addictions, both physical and emotional. It liberates us from slavery to chemicals and security, mostly by transforming our perception.

This is not a new method, nor is it a new problem. In fact, it is the central issue addressed by the Buddha nearly 2,500 years ago in Northern India. He noticed that everyone who lived experienced pain. He also noted that nothing people tried removed the pain, but actually made the suffering more acute. He says, "Birth is suffering, old age is suffering, illness is suffering, death is suffering; grief, lamentation, pain, affliction, and despair are suffering: to be united with what is unloved, to be separated from what is loved is suffering; not to obtain what is longed for is suffering." We can probably all attest to the truth of this, but the Buddha's great insight was to see the pain as a symptom of a greater underlying problem. The answer was not to numb the pain with chemicals or overwork, or to assuage it emotionally through others, sex, or compulsive religiosity, but to reach behind the symptom to the disease itself: a misperception of one's place in the universe.

The Buddha gave to us the promise of salvation in the Four Noble Truths: (1) There is suffering, (2) suffering has a cause, (3) suffering can cease, and (4) there is a way to make it cease.

We can all relate to the first truth, I am sure. But our revelation begins with the second. The cause of suffering is, according to the Buddhist tradition, a result of our "buying into" the illusion of consensus reality. Consensus reality tells us that we are separate creatures with no visible (and so, no actual) connection; we are millions of individual selves all looking out for "Number One." We are ultimately alone, and in our panic and insecurity, we clutch at what we think we need to maintain our status quo, and to improve it if we can.

The Buddha's great discovery is that consensus reality is inaccurate. He perceived that we are all a part of the great dance of the universe, all members of a great Self, and not millions of tiny, separate selves after all. As Buddhist scholar Hans Schumann writes of the Mahayana view, "Liberation is...to be achieved by the removal of the ignorance and by the realisation of the Absolute." Once I perceive that the universe is Me, I am transformed. I am no longer small nor alone. All of Creation is a unified body which rises and falls like waves on the ocean. What I think is me is just the result of a swell on the sea that circumstance has engineered. This swell will break and rejoin the body of the water from which it has, indeed, never been separated. Whatever happens to this body is of little consequence; it is not me. The universe in all its myriad forms that goes on forever is the eternal life of which I am a partaker. I am connected. I am One.

When we fully grasp this truth, we can move on to the third truth: suffering can cease. When we spend all our energy grasping after what we think our little self needs, we perpetuate the cycle of our suffering. But if we can understand that all we ever need is provided by the universe (since we *are* the universe), we have need of nothing. Lao Tzu says, "when we let go of everything, we have everything we need." Jesus told us to look at the flowers of the field and the birds of the air, they are provided for. Indeed, if everyone would awaken to this truth, there would be no grasping, no hoarding, no robbery, no greed, for there would be no hunger, and no poverty. For there really is enough for all.

The Twelve Steps in some way echo the Four Truths. The first step is merely to admit our suffering. The second is to recognize that we are not alone. To turn our will and trust over to a Higher Power is to have faith in something greater than our own, miniscule selves. It is to admit that we have been under the illusion of our isolation, when in fact we are much, much more than we thought we were. The Mahayana Buddhists would call the Universal Self the Cosmic Buddha, much as Christians would call it the Cosmic Christ. The "Us" that is bigger than us. The "Us" that is the *real* us.

If we can awaken to reality as it really is (the primary goal in Buddhist practice—"Buddha" means "awakened") we learn to trust the universe, eliminating desire and with it our neurotic compulsion to satisfy the cravings that lead us into the abyss of addiction.

Are We Just Born Bad?

Hsün Tzu and Augustine of Hippo in Comparison

We would, perhaps, be hard put to find two less likely figures for comparison than Hsün Tzu (298–238 BCE) and St. Augustine of Hippo (354–430 CE). They are from cultures totally alien to one another, at different times, and of considerable differences in philosophy. Yet each, independent of the other, taught an unpopular doctrine—that the intrinsic nature of humanity is evil. It is this seeming similarity and rash of differences with which this essay is concerned, and hopefully, we will show that even the similar teachings regarding human nature are, in fact, so dissimilar as to end any opinion of agreement.

Superficially, however, there is much in their distinct dramas from which we might draw many similarities. They were, for instance, both highly learned men, albeit they took different routes to their educations: Augustine was extensively schooled, while Hsün Tzu was largely self-taught. Both were figures of some degree of political prominence. As Bishop of Hippo, Augustine gained not insubstantial influence in regard to the emperor and the papacy. This, in fact, may be the sole reason Augustine's ideas were accepted despite their heinous pessimism. Hsün Tzu, while not gaining anything near Augustine's position, did gain the ear of some in power, notably King Hsün at the court in Ch'i, though the post was short-lived and Hsün Tzu had little success in propagating his ideas.[1] Both also engaged in heated literary debates with their philosophical opponents, the surviving texts providing some of the most exciting reading in the canons of each.

Superficiality aside, however, it is the opinion that human nature is intrinsically evil that suggests the comparison of these two worthy philosophers. Evil is not, for them, an acquired trait born of experience, but something present at birth. Hsün Tzu says, "The nature is that which is given by Heaven; you cannot learn it, you cannot acquire it by effort."[2] For Hsün Tzu, goodness is cultivated via ritual principles, which, if a man lacks them, "his behavior will be chaotic, and if he does not understand them, he will be wild and irresponsible. In fact, therefore, man in the state in which he is born possesses this tendency toward chaos and irresponsibility."[3] Augustine would agree that human nature is corrupt from birth, declaring that, although "we did not yet have individually created and apportioned forms in which to live as individuals" what did exist already was the "nature of the semen from which we were to be propagated." Elaine Pagels notes that it is Augustine's opinion that, due to human nature actually being inherited via the male, "every human being ever conceived through semen already is born contaminated with sin."[4] Augustine went so far as to declare that newborn infants were so corrupt as to be the very limbs of Satan![5] Hsün Tzu says, "Hence, any man who follows his nature and indulges his emotions will inevitably become involved in wrangling and strife, will violate the forms and rules of society, and will end as a criminal,"[6] a statement with which Augustine would no doubt whole-heartedly agree.

Both philosophers also agree that intervention is necessary to make anything useful out of Original Man. Goodness, for both men, is an acquired trait. Hsün Tzu writes, "a warped piece of wood must wait until it has been laid against the straightening board, steamed, and forced into shape before it can become straight, because by nature it is warped. Similarly, since man's nature is evil, he must wait for the ordering power of the sage kings and the transforming power of ritual principles; only then can he achieve order and conform to goodness."⁷ Augustine agrees, believing that humankind cannot be trusted to govern itself, because our very nature—indeed all of nature—has become corrupt.⁸ Pagels writes: "By insisting that humanity, ravaged by sin, now lies helplessly in need of outside intervention, Augustine's theory could not only validate secular power but justify as well the imposition of church authority—by force if necessary—as essential for human salvation."⁹

For Augustine, the intervention is the Church, which provides, in Chinese terms, sage rulers and ritual principles. For the Christian, this means baptism and indoctrination (in symbolic terms, the ruling Catholic hierarchy is seen as sort of sage-kings, or philosopher-kings, to use the Greek idea, though very rarely has the reality lived up to the expression). Passion, especially, for both men was a dead giveaway concerning humanity's intrinsic nature and continued corruption. For Augustine, sexual desire is the proof of universal original sin,¹⁰ to which Hsün Tzu might have responded with an emphatic "Man's emotions, man's emotions—they are very unlovely things indeed!"¹¹

Hsün Tzu resonates even with some of Augustine's more Neo-Platonic leanings. For instance, when Hsün Tzu writes "the mind gives meaning to impressions. It gives meaning to impressions, and only then, by means of the ear, can sound be known; by means of the eye, can forms be known.... When the five senses note something but cannot classify it, and the mind tries to identify it but fails to give it meaning, then one can only say that there is no knowledge."¹² While this is a long way from Plato's world of forms, or Augustine's parallel, the Mind of God,¹³ we can see the spark of parallel thinking. Hsün Tzu is saying that unless there is a corresponding archetype or idea in one's pre-existing mental schema, it is impossible to identify or classify any incoming data from the senses.

However much sympathy there might seem to be between these thinkers, however, they are also in many ways polar opposites. Hsün Tzu is not nearly so pessimistic regarding human nature. Yes, it is evil, but as Fung Yu-Lan points out, "man at the same time possesses intelligence, and...this intelligence makes it possible for him to become good."[14] Indeed, almost like a mantra, the text of Hsün Tzu's book repeats, "Man's nature is evil; goodness is the result of conscious activity."[15] H.H. Dubs, in his *Hsüntze, the Moulder of Ancient Confucianism*, almost draws Augustine into the discussion by mentioning his ideological heir, John Calvin, when he writes, "With Hsün Tzu this doctrine did not mean that human nature was totally depraved and without any hope, as in the teaching of Calvin, but rather just the opposite; because human nature tended to evil, each man must all the more work to develop his own nature towards the right. Human nature merely tends to evil; it has an infinite capacity for development in the direction of good as well."[16]

The result of this thinking is that anyone who wills it can cultivate the good in him/herself. Even the most common of persons can become a sage.[17] As Hsün Tzu himself writes, "if the man in the street applies himself to training and study, concentrates his mind and will, and considers and examines things carefully, continuing his efforts over a long period of time and accumulating good acts without stop, then he can achieve a godlike understanding and form a triad with Heaven and earth. The sage is a man who has arrived where he has through the accumulation of good acts."[18] So, by this philosophy, anyone has it in their power to be perfect and virtuous. Dubs makes the point that this doctrine is "the nearest that Confucianism came to the Christian teaching of the infinite worth of every individual."[19] I can only guess that Mr. Dubs has not been reading Augustine, for the good Saint's thoughts on this matter are as diametrically opposed as is humanly possible.

Augustine believed that God arbitrarily divides humankind into the elect and the reprobate. This is fair since, because human nature is evil, we are all wicked anyway and deserving of damnation. So if God chooses to spare some, it is the result of his infinite mercy, and none have any right to complain.[20] As Bertrand Russell puts it, "the elect go to heaven because God chooses to make them the objects of His mercy: they are virtuous because they are elect, not elect because they are virtuous."[21] For Augustine, humankind has no power to make itself virtuous. He says, "the rational creature...has been so made that it cannot itself be the good by which it is made happy."[22] Augustine would not have approved of Hsün Tzu's view at all, nor did he approve when a young monk named Pelagius challenged him that his doctrine was too severe. Pelagius thought that people still had free will and the power to live without sin; unlikely but possible (with which Hsün Tzu also would have concurred). For his pains, Pelagius was excommunicated, and the Church swung towards Augustine's position.[23]

Another great difference between our thinkers is their cosmology. Augustine's God was personal and quite anthropomorphic, while Hsün Tzu's was impersonal, the Tao, the Way of Heaven, more of a principle than a person. In his estimation, "The Universe was righteous in its very constitution, and needed not God or spiritual beings to insure the supremacy of good over evil."[24] Where Augustine is totally dependent on outside divine agency, since no human being can do good without grace—"a grace which the Almighty deliberately withholds from the majority of His creatures."[25] Hsün Tzu is equally independent, feeling that any attempts to venture beyond the human, knowable realm are pointless and futile.[26] Help, for Hsün Tzu, might be necessary, but is obtainable from human sources. As he says, "since man's nature is evil, it must wait for the instructions of a teacher before it can become upright, and for the guidance of ritual principles before it can become orderly."[27] Yu-Lan points out that Mencius, unlike his rival, did seek supernatural intervention, saying that "in order to become a sage, one must 'know Heaven.' But Hsün Tzu maintains, on the contrary: 'it is only the sage who does not seek to know Heaven.'"[28]

Hsün Tzu laments that the sorry state of humankind is owing to the absence of the sage-king. For "were there to be such a sage-king, he would use his political authority to unify the minds of the people, and lead them to the true way of life in which there is not place or need for disputation and argument."[29] This is not necessarily so, as Augustine's example amply points out. Until the emperor Constantine converted to Christianity, Rome was a pagan state and Christians lived in fear for their lives. Yet, when the state itself became Christian, suddenly politics was subservient to doctrine, and the West saw the rise of great political power in the Church. Suddenly, the sages—or priest-kings—were in power, and, like their pagan counterparts before them, they used their power in despicable ways to enforce the "unity of the minds of the people," with unrestrained barbarity. (One is inclined to believe that Hsün Tzu's sage-king exists only in Plato's world of forms.)

Humanity's place in the universe is also a point of contention. The Vatican just recently pardoned Galileo for his "heretical" doctrine (that the Earth was not the center of the universe). This anthropocentrism is at the heart of nearly all Western philosophy and theology. Such hubris is not, however, so widely accepted in the East. Hsün Tzu himself says "The ten thousand beings are only one corner of the Way. One species of being is only one corner of the ten thousand beings. The stupid man is only one corner of one species. He himself believes that he understands the Way, though of course he does not."[30] Such wisdom seems lost on the West, as often the most obvious is. Philosopher R.A. Marus comments on Augustine's attitude toward nature when he writes, "The world of nature was not in itself an object of particular interest in Augustine."[31] In fact, Michael Planyi has written that Augustine "destroyed interest in science all over Europe for a thousand years," because for him science "contributed nothing to the pursuit of salvation."[32] Such doctrines of Augustine would quickly and pervasively sway all of Europe and Western civilization to his peculiar brand of pessimism, so unlike the surprisingly hopeful stance of Hsün Tzu.

Thus, the result of closer comparison reveals more striking differences than the initially apparent similarities suggest. And, in retrospect, it is perhaps unfortunate that the fortunes of these two thinkers were not reversed. For while Augustine went on to become the favored interpreter of St. Paul, and thus won not only sainthood, but academic immortality, Hsün Tzu was not so fortunate. Mencius won out as the prime interpreter of Confucius, and Hsün Tzu, just like Pelagius, Julian, and many other philosophical opponents of Augustine, was condemned. Though they are not forgotten, they are certainly not held in the same esteem.

For more on St. Augustine, read "The Naughty Bishop of Hippo" on page 195.

NOTES

1 Watson, Burton, trans. *Hsün Tzu: Basic Writings* (New York: Columbia University Press, 1963), p. 2.

2 *Ibid.*, p. 158.

3 *Ibid.*, p. 162.

4 Pagels, Elaine. *Adam, Eve, and the Serpent* (New York: Random House, 1988), p. 109.

5 Russell, Bertrand, quoting Augustine. *A History of Western Philosophy* (New York: Simon and Schuster, 1945), p. 365.

6 Watson, p. 157.

7 *Ibid.*, p. 164.

8 Pagels, p.145.

9 *Ibid.*, p. 124-5.

10 *Ibid.*, p. xviii.

11 Watson, p. 168.

12 Yu-Lan, Fung. *A Short History of Chinese Philosophy* (New York: Macmillan, 1948), p. 151.

13 Copleston, Frederick, S.J. *A History of Philosophy, Volume II* (New York: Image, 1962), p. 73..

14 Yu-Lan, p. 145.

15 Watson, p. 157.

16 Dubs, H.H. *Hsüntze: The Moulder of Ancient Confucianism* (London: Arthur Probsthain, 1927), p. 77.

17 Yu-Lan, p. 145.

18 Watson, p. 167.

19 Dubs, p. 84.

20 Russell, p. 362.

21 *Ibid.*, p. 274.

22 Copleston, p. 81.

23 Russell, Bertrand; Al Seckel, ed. *On God and Religion* (Buffalo: Prometheus, 1986), p. 243.

24 Dubs, p. 56.

25 Azkoul, Michael. *The Influence of Augustine of Hippo on the Orthodox Church* (Lewiston: Edwin Mellen Press, 1990), p. 207.

26 Watson, p. 8.

27 *Ibid.*, p. 158.

28 Yu-Lan, p. 144.

29 *Ibid.*, p. 153.

30 Watson, p. 87.

31 Fox, Matthew. *Original Blessing* (Santa Fe: Bear & Co., 1983), p. 75.

32 *Ibid.*, p. 11.

Power:

the Greatest Temptation

In *Das Rheingold*, the first opera in Wagner's Ring cycle, the action begins when the Rheinmaidens, the daughters of the river, are teasing the dwarf, Alberich. They seem to get a great deal of pleasure out of his frustration, as they lure him on romantically and then spurn his advances. Eventually they up the ante by telling him their great secret, that the gold that lies beneath the river can be had by anyone who forswears love. Of course, Alberich is such a little bundle of sexual angst that they can't imagine in a million years that he might be tempted to do that. It is just that much more to tease him with.

But Alberich surprises them. He swears off forever the love of women, and seizes the river's gold for himself. And from it he forges a ring of power that can control the fate of even the gods.

Now about this time Wotan, the king of the gods, is facing a dilemma. He promised the frost giants the goddess Freya if they would build his castle. The giants have finished the castle, and they have come to collect Freya. Instantly the gods realize this was a *bad* mistake, because Freya's apples are the source of their immortality. No Freya, no apples. No apples, no youth.

Thor suggests that they simply kill the giants, and tempting as this idea is, Wotan nixes it for one very good reason: he is God and he must obey his own rules. The Staff of Law he holds prevents that course of action. Panicked, the gods invoke Loki, the trickster god, who is not on anybody's side. Loki tells them about the Rheingold and about the dwarf Alberich, and suggests that the giants might take this gold instead of Freya. And, since Alberich stole it in the first place, it wouldn't really be stealing to take from a thief. This Wotan does, and Alberich curses the ring and all who wear it.

Not heeding this curse, Wotan decides to give all the gold to the ice giants, *except* for the ring, which he intends to keep for himself. But then the frost giants enter and agree to the trade. However, they are not happy with simply the pile of gold; they want the ring, too.

Mysteriously, another figure appears, Erda, the earth goddess, who prophesies that they must surrender the ring or they are doomed, doomed, doomed. Wotan struggles with this, but finally, he throws the ring on the pile, and the exchange is made.

One of the frost giants no sooner receives the booty than he kills his brother giant over it, proving Erda's warning about the accursed ring.

In this story, well known to opera lovers everywhere, the characters are faced with numerous temptations. Alberich is tempted to wield power over the earth, to take the earth's treasures for his own, without considering the consequences of his actions. Thor and Wotan are tempted to wield power over other beings when they consider simply killing the giants in order to get their way. And finally, Wotan is tempted to grasp power over even divine beings, and indeed the universe, by clinging to the dread ring of power.

So we see three types of temptation in this story: to grasp power over the earth, over other people, and over the gods. To the gods' credit, they do not give in to their temptations. But the poor dwarf Alberich is not so discerning, and he suffers for it.

It is interesting to note how often the mythologies of diverse cultures run parallel, because when we come to the story of Jesus' journey into the wilderness, we find the same pattern of temptations.

First, Satan tempts Jesus to wield power over the natural world and turn stones into bread. He tempts him to use his "magic powers" for his own comfort, to impose his will upon his environment in order to get what he wants.

Later, Satan tempts Jesus with temporal power, power over all the peoples of the world. All Jesus has to do is swear his loyalty and the world is his; all the nations, all the wealth, all the power. All he has to do is sell his soul. How many people do you know who think that this is a bargain?

Finally, Satan tempts Jesus to wield power over God, to force God to save him. Satan tells him to jump off the temple, for God was sure to send angels to break his fall and thereby prove to all those in the crowded city square below that he was the Son of God. Wield power over God?? Surely by this point anyone could see the absurdity of Satan's temptation, the desperation he must have been feeling to propose this one. "Wield power over God, so that you can put on a good show."

No. Jesus refuses. He will have none of it. Jesus will not wield his power over the earth. He will not wield power over the people. He will not wield power over God. That is not Christ's way. Paul says that he "emptied himself of power and took on the form of a servant." It was by abdicating power that Jesus performed his redeeming work. It was by rejecting power that he confounded not just Satan, but the religious and civil authorities, and yes, Jesus continues to confound us today.

These temptations are universal. The temptation to wield power over nature is a common one for us in modernity and post-modernity: we want the world to conform to our desires, we want people to change in order to suit us; we want to pervert and distort the natural world to please us. We want to change stones to bread. And why not? After all, a shopping mall is much more pleasing to look at than a forest, isn't it? Like Alberich, it is tempting to want to wrest from the earth the things we desire, regardless of the consequences. And yet the venerable scripture of native China, the *Tao Te Ching* tells us, "Do you think you can change the world? If you try, you will destroy it, like too much poking at a frying fish!" Jesus says "no" to this sort of power-over, and unlike Alberich, so should we.

Likewise, grasping power that is not ours over our fellow human beings is no better. Satan promised Jesus the throne of the world. Each of us has been tempted to violence or guile against another person, especially if that person "deserves" it! Yet, our sacred writings say that this is clearly evil. Thou shalt not kill, thou shalt not steal, thou shalt not covet thy neighbor's wife, or anything that is his. No, Wotan and Thor chose rightly. Like Jesus, they held firm to the Staff of the Law, and refused.

Finally, trying to seize power over God is the greatest evil. In biblical terms, this is called sorcery, attempting to coerce divinity by magical or other means. And though most of us might say, "Oh, but I don't know anyone like that," one really only needs to look as far as the nearest mirror. We all, in our times of great need and anguish, attempt to bargain and deal with God. We try in our futile and pathetic ways to sway the fate of the universe for our own comfort, and it is almost always a bad idea. Jesus will not tempt God, will not force God's hand. Erda warns that wielding such power will bring ruin, and Wotan, in his wisdom, surrenders it.

What is it within us that desires power? Is it the discomfort of the times when we have felt powerless, and an urge to compensate, or perhaps to protect us from ever feeling that way again? What is it in human nature that compels us to reach for the forbidden fruit of power over another?

As I walked the block and a half to my neighborhood's polling place last Tuesday, I found that I faced a great internal dilemma. Oh, the various referenda and propositions were easy enough for me to decide, but when it came to selecting a presidential candidate for last week's primaries, I just felt all weird inside.

You see, I just don't think that anyone who *wants* to be president should be allowed to. Whatever the relative merits that each of the four main-party candidates may possess, they are all professional politicians, masters of the greased palm and back-room dealmaking. The idea that any of them legitimately *deserves* the office seems ludicrous to me.

Power does weird things to people's heads. Give someone a little power, and they instantly suffer under the bizarre delusion that they have a *right* to that power. Suddenly the need of one outweighs the needs of many, and the toboggan slide down the slippery slope to damnation has begun. It is the temptation to wield power over other beings that lies at the core of the dark heart of humankind.

In Tolkien's *Lord of the Rings* trilogy, which borrows much from Wagner's story, it is only the fact that the Dark Lord cannot even conceive of Frodo and Sam's plan that allows them to succeed in their quest. The Dark Lord can not bring himself to believe that anyone would willingly part with the ring of power, let alone destroy it. And that of course, is what Frodo and Sam have set out to do. To destroy the instrument of power-over. To say "no" to that temptation. Like Jesus, like Wotan and Thor, like Frodo and Sam, we are called to do the same, but as we all know, this is often easier said than done.

A few months ago, I told you that I had been nominated by several sources to be made a bishop in my religious community, the Old Catholic succession. Now, the last thing I ever wanted to be was a bishop! But nonetheless, the idea is tempting, because I feel that, by and large, most bishops do a pretty poor job in executing their duties. And I have just enough hubris to think that I might possibly be able to do better. I prayed about the decision, and the answer I received from God was "Yes, but not now." So I have put the bishop issue on the back burner, and in a year, or two years, or five years, when it comes up again, I will pray about it again. But when I told one friend about my decision, someone who had been advocating me for the "promotion," he was astounded. "Now, I *know* you should be consecrated a bishop," he said, "because no one has ever said 'no' before."

As I reflect on today's reading, I feel a little glow of warmth inside. Perhaps I passed some kind of test. I was offered the gift of power over my fellow clergy, and I declined. I know there will be other tests tomorrow, and I know that one day God may call me to fulfill my responsibility towards my community in the episcopal role. But I pray that even in a position of power, as Wotan was, as many of you are and have been, I will be able to foreswear it. That, like Jesus, I will be able to empty myself of the power of my office and take the form of a servant, whether I am wearing a miter or not.

In this church, we have constructed a laboratory for just such experiments with power. Here we have kept the traditional roles of pastor and layperson, but we have turned the power dynamic on its ear. It is very clear that in this community, Richard and I serve *you*. It is very clear who wears the miter in this church: the voting members. It is my belief that God is calling all spiritual communities to consensus power arrangements. After all, the scripture says that "the valleys will be exalted and the mountains made low." The promise of America bears this out: the kings have been cast from their thrones, and the people rule through democracy. And in this church, the bishops have been stripped of their power, and it is the laity who rule.

It is tempting to grasp after power. But whether that takes the form of power over the earth, power over other humans, or power over God, it is always wrong. We are often sent into the wilderness where we face grave decisions. That is the human lot in life. But it is up to us whether we will be ministered to by the angels.

PART THREE

What Religions Tell Us About the Spiritual Journey

The Primal Spiritual Journey

In the Bhagavad Gita, one of the holiest scriptures of the Hindu religion, Prince Arjuna is surveying a battlefield. On one side are his brothers and the many mercenaries they were able to raise during their long exile in the forest. Leading the opposing armies are Arjuna's cousins, who stole his brothers' thrones. He also sees his lifelong friends and his teachers in the opposing army. Suddenly despair overwhelms him, and he drops his bow to the dirt and falls to his knees, crying out to God.

Fortunately for Arjuna, God is not only nearby, he is driving his chariot. Krishna, the incarnation of the ultimate godhead, feels compassion for his friend, and seeks to comfort him. "What is the matter?" Krishna asks, even though, as God, he probably knows. Like any good therapist, Krishna knows that we have to work through these things for ourselves sometimes.

"How can I go through with this?" Arjuna wailed. "How can I go out and kill my friends, my teachers, my own family? How can I destroy the very people I fight to save?"

And then and there on the battlefield, Krishna comes down from his perch in the chariot, and while the armies on both sides bristle for the horns to blow and the battle to commence, Krishna gives Arjuna an introductory course in cosmology.

"Do you see all these people?" He asks. "They are all just a part of me. That general is a fingernail on my hand, this whole battlefield is as my thigh. All things in heaven and earth are a part of me. And here's the secret: I am the eternal God. I never die. And since all things are a part of me, and I never die, nothing ever really dies."

Then Krishna reveals himself to Arjuna in all his glory, a kaleidoscopic vision that leaves Arjuna disoriented and breathless. Afterwards, Krishna entreats his friend, saying, "This battle is part of a story which must be played out for the good of the universe. Go and do your duty. Yes, go on out and kill, but do it with a twinkle in your eye, because everything is me, and I cannot be killed."

Arjuna takes courage from his friend's impromptu philosophy lesson and joins his army for the battle about to commence. Arjuna discovers that he is, in fact, not really, foundationally Arjuna. His being Arjuna is revealed to be an illusion. In reality, he is a part of Krishna, he *is* Krishna, and that moment of realization is his salvation.

While there are certainly disturbing aspects to this story, it clearly illustrates a kernel of truth which one can find at the heart of every one of the world's religions, Christianity included.

I am a great fan of Carl Jung. Now, while the man doubtless had certifiable clay feet, and would be the first to admit to his own shadow, he gave scholars of religion an inestimable gift in that he provided a new, psychological vocabulary to describe religious experience. The advantage of this is that, by using Jung's categories and terminology, we are able to see what is going on in a religion's teachings without getting bogged down in proprietary terminology or dogma. And the amazing result of this is that we are able to see just how much we have in common.

In Jung's system, we human beings suffer as much as we do because we think that we are our egos. As long as I identify with my ego, I am going to have a difficult time because the ego needs to think that it is in control, it is terrified at the prospect of its extinction, it has a great investment in my believing that "I" and "it" are synonymous. But deep within ourselves there is another

Self, a Self with a capital "S." This Self is synonymous with the universe itself, we might even call it God if we were to revert to religious terminology. This Self speaks to us "between the cracks" in our consciousness. It takes over when we sleep and dances through our dreams, it shows itself in moments of creative insight, it leaps out during psychotic episodes. The Self is the great unconscious well from which we all draw. Jung called it "the collective unconscious," and as such it is common to all peoples in every place and time.

The spiritual journey, according to Jung, is for us to realize that the ego is not us. It is a pretender to the throne. It is a "persona," a false face that we develop in early childhood to erect a barrier between ourselves and the unconscious so that we can distinguish between fantasy and reality and become functional in the world. As such, the ego is a very useful tool and is developmentally appropriate. But although a pacifier is appropriate when a child is one or two, it becomes problematic when a child is five. Just so, the ego is important when we are emerging out of the unconscious into the material world, but as we grow into adulthood, the ego's tyranny becomes apparent. We learn the hard way that we are not the only being in the universe, that others have feelings and needs, and that very often our own desires must be set aside so that others might have their most basic needs met.

That is called "growing up." But if the ego has its way, this process will be circumvented before we actually get to the bottom of it all. For if we keep going in this line of inquiry we are forced to ask the question, "If the ego is just a part of who I am, who am I really?" And Jung's answer to this is that our true identity is the capital "S" Self, the ground of all being.

This is the meaning behind the promise of immortality every religion holds out. So long as we identify with our ego, we will die. But if we find our identity in a larger and more permanent entity, then our survival beyond the death of this fragile body is assured. Let's look at some religions, and I'll show you what I mean.

In Judaism, one is not so much an individual as a part of the family, the tribe, the people of Israel. Judaism is one of the least transcendent religions in that it promises no survival of the ego after death, but exists to ensure the survival of the tribe through time, resting in God's promise that they will thrive and endure. Judaism invites its followers to divorce their identity from their individual egos, and asks them to invest their identities in the Jewish people as a whole. A man or woman might die, but Israel never dies. Thus, anyone who invests his or her identity in the Jewish people achieves a kind of immortality.

In Buddhism, the ego is revealed to be our "false face," and so long as we continue in the delusion that the "false face" is who we are, we suffer. But when we recognize our "true face" as being identical with all of being, we accept things as they are, and our suffering vanishes. We discover that we all have "Buddha nature" and that this common nature connects us not only across all national, racial, and social boundaries, but to all beings.

In Islam, the ego is forced into "submission," which is the meaning of the word "Islam." Muslims submit their will to the greater will of Allah, and strive to serve as conduits for the divine will. Islamic mystics go even further, discovering in their ecstatic trances that "Allah and I are one." The ego is thus defeated, living in submission to the true will governing the universe.

In Christianity, Jesus says that we must "be born again," we must experience a shift in our consciousness. Jesus said that a seed must fall to the earth and die before the kernel of wheat can take root and spring forth with new life. It is not hard to see the seed as the ego, and the resulting, triumphant plant as the true Self finding expression in one's life. St. Paul describes this as "putting on Christ." "No longer do I live," Paul tells us, "But Christ lives through me." In Christianity, believers become part of the Body of Christ. Christ is our new identity, in Christ we "live and move and have our being." And because Christ never dies, so we, too, when we have put on Christ, have put on immortality.

What made Jesus, and the Buddha, and all of the world's great mystics so profound and powerful in their teaching, is that they were able to make this shift in identity. In our gospel reading today, Jesus goes into the wilderness, the symbolic place of spiritual dryness, where we are all vulnerable to temptation. There he is met by Satan, who sets before him three temptations. Let's look at each of them. In the first, Satan tempts him to suspend the laws of the universe in order to turn stones into bread. We might say that Satan suggests that he violate the integrity of Creation in order to fill his own belly. "Who cares about the whole," he is saying, "When you are hungry?" In other words, "Why not feed the ego at the expense of the Self?"

The second temptation is larger in scope. Satan shows Jesus the kingdoms of the world and promises him dominion over all of them if Jesus will only bow to Satan's authority. Satan is definitely making a play for Jesus' ego here, but Jesus is not identified with the ego. Jesus is identified with God. As God is already lord of all the world, and, as Jesus says, "I and the Father are One," what Satan is really offering is a demotion, not a promotion. Again, Satan wants Jesus to feed his ego at the expense of the Self, and Jesus is not biting.

In the third, Satan is even craftier, for in this temptation Satan plays on Jesus' ego's need to be accepted and believed. If the people see a miraculous rescue, if they see Jesus being borne down to earth by angels, surely they will believe him. Satan is tempting him to put his money where his mouth is, to prove his legitimacy to his followers and perhaps even to himself. But Jesus has no need to prove anything. Jesus is not his ego. Jesus is God. The shift in identity has already been made in Jesus' mind, and Satan's temptations cannot touch him.

We would do well to follow Jesus' example, here. We, too, can find our identity in God. For most of the violence in our world is the result of fear, of people needing to protect the things their egos say they "need" to survive. But if we were able to truly shift our identity from this hollow shell that will die to the Whole that will never die, our actions might be quite different. We would not cheat one another, for we would be conscious that we are a part of one another, and if I cheat you, I cheat myself. We would have no poor or homeless people because we would provide for others, knowing that providing for others is simply providing for ourselves. When Jesus said, "Whatsoever you do to the least of these my brethren, you do unto me," he was speaking from precisely this perspective. And he was speaking a much more literal truth than people normally associate with this verse.

Like Jesus, we are beset by such temptations every day, in ways big and small. How we respond to them will largely be determined by our identity. Who are you? Are you this small bag of bones and flesh in whom the light of consciousness will soon be extinguished, never to flame again? Or are you the universe, which lives forever? The choice is yours to make, and if the religions of the universe are any guide, then hear them, for on this matter, they speak with one voice. You are not your body. You are not your mind. You are infinitely more than you can ever comprehend, and your story has no end. If you can make that shift in consciousness, if you can "put on the mind of Christ," if you can recognize your true face, then, my friends, Satan, death, and hell cannot touch you. And that is good news, indeed.

Hindu Myth and Paradigm Shift

"**M**yths are stories that make sense of our lives." This is the only thing I remember from my freshman philosophy class. It was a great revelation and it began a process of thinking that significantly changed my world view. It is common today to refer to a world-view as a paradigm. The paradigm, the belief structure on which I hang the disparate parts of my life, has shifted to where it is no longer necessary for me to have all the answers, or to insist that everyone have *my* answers. I have come to recognize that religious and cultural pluralism is not only a more just way of living, but an essential element of a holy life. What occurred in me was a shift of my former paradigm to a better-functioning one.

What those who have experienced this shift on a personal level seem to be working toward is effectively facilitating this shift on a larger scale; even a global scale. This involves a drastic change in people's thinking, which will frighten some and will therefore be a difficult thing to accomplish. It will also be dangerous: ask Socrates, Martin Luther, Copernicus, or Jesus.

Such a massive shift occurred in the Hindu religion 25 hundred years ago. Many people have the impression that Hinduism is a polytheistic religion, an understandable mistake since there are nearly as many known Hindu gods as there are living Hindus. But Hinduism is not polytheistic, it is monotheistic. There is only one God, Brahman. In fact, for the Hindu, that's really *all* there is. All of creation is part of Brahman; including the stars, the gods, and us.

Primitive Hinduism of the Vedic period (3,000—500 B.C.) *was* polytheistic. There was the chief of the gods, Indra, whose fierceness in battle and erotic exploits were unchallenged; there was Agni, the fire-god, who knew all things; and countless others. But something happened; there came a time when the old theology was no longer adequate to answer the difficult questions the Hindus faced. They began to perceive that the gods were all extensions—masks—of the one God.

This was a profound paradigm shift, and it did not happen overnight. At first it was a great and holy secret doctrine whispered from master to disciple. But eventually the shift was made on a popular level, partly because there was a story:

Brahman, the one God, had just seen to it that Indra and the other gods won their latest battle. Indra and the others were taking credit, bragging about their bravery and ferocity, when Brahman appeared to them. They were a bit taken aback and said to each other, "Who is this being that fills us with such awe?" They pushed Agni out in front and told him to find out (he was, after all, supposed to know everything).

"Who are you?" asked the one God. "I am the god of fire," Agni answered. "What power do you possess?" Agni replied proudly, "I can burn all things on the earth." Brahman placed a piece of straw before him and said, "Burn this." Agni tried and tried, but couldn't even raise a decent smolder. Agni returned to the other gods shaken and bewildered.

Next the gods sent Vayu, the god of the air. "I am Vayu, god of air and space," he announced when he stood in front of the mysterious being. "What are your powers?" Brahman asked. "I can carry off all the earth in a whirlwind." Brahman held forth the same piece of straw and said, "Blow this away." Vayu too, returned unsuccessful.

Finally Indra, chief of the gods, squared his jaw and ran toward the being, but Brahman disappeared. All the gods were speechless with wonder, for they knew they had seen the Supreme Spirit, the source of their being.

Through this story, the Hindu faith successfully maneuvered a paradigm shift, from one of tribal polytheism to a tolerant monotheism. It was revealed Truth, and it was through the power of the myth that it was translated into daily life.

Hinduism was in a crucial time of uncertainty and change that took place during what has been termed "the axial period." If we are going to survive into the next era, desperate changes in our way of living and perceiving must occur; we must effect a paradigm shift in our culture. The facts have already been provided. Physicists like Stephen Hawking, Fritzjof Capra, and Brian Swimme have given us the facts about our history, about what and why we are. Their books, *A Brief History of Time, The Tao of Physics* and *The Universe is a Green Dragon*, respectively, have made the information understandable and have filled us with a justifiable sense of holy awe. We in Creation Spirituality have been calling this the New Story, but what we really need is a new Myth. Are we ready to move beyond anthropocentrism to a degree that our myths need not include anthropomorphic characters? This is an important question.

Our facts are here, but where are the storytellers? Only a myth can touch us where we are the most human; only a myth can break down our divisive barriers; only a myth can unite our souls. Only a myth can speak to us on an archetypal level that will bring the danger and the hope home to each of us. Only a myth can make sense of our lives.

Courage for Creative Theology

O f all the many religions of the world I have had the privilege to explore and study, none has captured my heart and imagination as profoundly as Hinduism. Hinduism is frightening to many people, and this is quite understandable. It is a kaleidoscope of ever-evolving ideas about the Divine. There are nearly as many historical Hindu gods as there are living Hindus. This is not a problem for the Hindu, because in his or her universe there is no thing, in physical space or in the imagination, that is not God. This is incredibly important, because what it provides for the believer is infinite creative liberty where the mind and spirit are concerned. As for material existence, philosophical Hinduism is fairly firm in its devotion to nonviolence, but in the realm of the creative drive that is our inheritance as beings made in the God's image, its bounds are unlimited.

This is at first a frightening thought. Indeed, a terrifying thought to the fundamentalist element in most traditions. Growing up in a conservative Protestant denomination, I would quickly be seized with terror if I happened to have a thought contrary to the accepted religious formula and would hastily ask God's forgiveness over and over to the point of despair—so vivid for me were the threats of eternal damnation awaiting heretics who do not keep their imaginations in check! We were taught to resist "unorthodox" ideas and were discouraged from allowing curiosity to bring us into contact with others who had such ideas. Not too long ago, it was with empathy and understanding that I first read of C.G. Jung's boyhood vision of God defecating on the cathedral. Such thoughts devastated me as a child, and I felt helpless in preventing them, thinking myself soiled and sinful.

But I have come to see that it is not ungodly to allow our imaginations to roam; and in fact, it is most imperative that they do. For the unfettered Hindu, this great liberty has fostered what I have come to believe is the most theologically advanced faith tradition known to humankind. For, as we Christians juggle and shuffle our traditional formulas, searching for new combinations in the puzzle of our faith that will provide answers to our present situations, the Hindu visionaries have transcended all formulas and christened all the universe as sacred in every conceivable form of matter, mind, and spirit. To allow the mind to soar to unprecedented heights, to journey into unexplored territory is not for the Hindu a sin and a threat to one's eternal security, but an ecstatic exploration of the infinite mind of God.

What do we gain, then, as Christians, in exploring this most alien faith tradition? What gifts do Shiva, Vishnu, and the rest of the Hindu pantheon bear to us in our communion with their faithful? The liberty to soar. Jeremy Taylor has said that "either the universe is a safe place to play or it isn't." With Jeremy, I believe it *is* a safe place to play. What is called for from us is courage. We have been unwitting captives in a foreign land that has raised us to suppress our abilities, to destroy our inheritances, and to deny the freedom that should be ours through the Gospel. And like the Israelites, newly liberated from Egypt, we have a choice to make: we can follow the Spirit as she leads us into the promised land that God intends, which will involve getting used to a whole new conceptual terrain—indeed a new paradigm already unfolding in the collective consciousness of our race—or we can cling to what we know, and with the fundamentalists of our traditions, harden our hearts and remember with fondness the leeks and onions we knew in an age of barbarism and slavery.

If we do not go forward, then we damn ourselves and our children—and our children's children—to a joyless subsistence in a wasteland of our own creation. And we can be reasonably sure that our choice will affect more than a mere 40 years of our planet's history. It will decide its destiny.

It is not dangerous to dream. We are in danger if we fail in our responsibility to follow the Spirit into places we know not of, even deserts or dungeons. And we must not fear to make mistakes: we must trust that the One who has created us is also faithful to shape and correct us, as the potter revealed to Jeremiah. Our sojourners in the Spirit in the Hindu tradition have already dared to dream, whereas we have not yet begun, even though the apostle Paul told us so long ago that there is "neither depth nor height...that can ever separate us from the love of God" (Rom 8). The Hindus have liberated their imaginations; yet we have not, even though the apostle revealed to us our freedom in Christ to exercise our Divine right as co-creators of the Universe (Gal 5). Our Hindu brethren have found God in all that is conceivable, whereas we have not yet found the eyes to see this, even though we have already heard the Psalmist and the mystics say that there is no place in the universe where God is not (Ps 39). For what have we to fear, when there is no place we go alone?

I do not deny that this can be scary; I still scare myself, such as when I first read Matthew Fox's *The Coming of the Cosmic Christ*, and it occurred to me that the second person of the Trinity includes me! But we must remember that the heroes of our faith faced identical opposition, both from within themselves and from without. We must be willing to suffer the scorn of our tradition's leaders even unto death, as did Jesus and St. Joan. We must dare to dream of justice, as did Susan B. Anthony and Martin Luther King, Jr. And we must have the courage and humility to receive the gifts our sister traditions bring to us in peace as we dream of being, and learn to become, a planet full of a People of Faith.

Bear Each Others' Burdens

A s a child, I read about people who believed that by rubbing a stone on their warts, the malady could be discarded when the stone was cast away. "How stupid," I thought, in my third-grade Eurocentric arrogance.

One thing I've learned since is not to dismiss the concepts I've found in Native religions, but to come to them with profound respect and a recognition that the ideas and rituals speak to the very heart of my own being, and in fact are themselves central to the faith I embrace and practice, though adorned with centuries of Christian spirituality and tradition.

This practice of transferring evil, sickness, and sin from the afflicted to something else, be it an inanimate object, an animal or another human, is found around the world, in both Native traditions and in most of the major world religions. In southern India a village practice is to lay hands upon a calf while reciting a litany of sins upon the animal, which is then driven into the wilderness, carrying with it the people's sins. This is nearly identical to the Israelite ritual found in the Torah concerning the scapegoat, and, similarly, Muslims in the Middle Ages rid themselves of plague by leading a camel through the village and then sacrificing it in a sacred place. In India a holy man, for a certain fee, will bear the sins of another and exile himself to take them away forever. This is a central concept in Christianity, where Jesus, the divine scapegoat or lamb, willingly bore our sins himself.

It is not uncommon in Native religions for a sickness to be borne away by another. A Celtic healer may take the sickness upon herself to the relief of the afflicted. (In fact, a woman, Agnes Sampson, was put to death for just such a ministry in 1590.)

What do we make of such a ministry today? Is this superstition? Are such occasions miracles? Can they actually occur?

A story is told of the famous Oxford apologist, C.S. Lewis, whose wife was suffering so terribly from terminal cancer that she was unable to rest. Lewis, it is said, took and bore her pain for an hour, himself experiencing the agony of the disease while his wife sank into a much needed sleep.

I was incredulous upon hearing this story for the first time, until I came across the work of the great Anglican mystic and author Charles Williams, who, in his novel *Descent Into Hell,* describes a character who offers to carry the paranoid fear of a young woman so that she might have the strength to face what she must. The young woman rejects his bizarre offer, humiliated, "Would I push my burden onto anybody else?" she replies. "Not if you insist on making a universe for yourself," she is answered. "If you want to disobey and refuse the laws that are common to us all, if you want to live in pride and division and anger, you can. But if you will be part of the best of us, and live and laugh and be ashamed with us, then you must be content to be helped." As the novel continues, she finally consents and is so overwhelmed with the grace of her surrender that she herself mystically travels to the aid of an ancestor several hundred years past at his martyrdom, and bears much of his pain as he is burned at the stake. So she had entered into communion. She can receive, and also willingly and in love, bear the pain of others.

I thought of this as so much interesting fantasy until a friend offered to receive my disabling worry over an approaching event. I laughed nervously, incredulously. He insisted that he was willing to share my burden of worry. I was amazed that I was clinging so desperately to this affliction. I confronted myself, and in a few seconds I was able to let it go. "Okay," I said to my friend, "Please help me." Instantly a wave passed over me, and the burden was lessened. My friend had indeed helped me and enabled me to meet my fear with courage.

Similarly, Yoruba priestess and ICCS faculty member Luisah Teish, in her book *Jambalaya*, relates an experience in which she was so sick she could hardly move to do anything to help relieve her suffering. Making a cup of herb tea seemed an impossibly exhausting endeavor. She says she was "too sick to heal my self...and too stubborn to die." She goes on: I remember asking the question, "What would [Momma] do if her child was this sick?"

"Some time passed; then I got up. As my feet hit the floor, I noticed varicose veins in my legs (which I do not have), and my muscles were not sore. I stood up and felt my hips much larger than they are.... It seemed as if I were wearing my mother's body!"

Teish went to the kitchen and prepared the home remedies Momma would have and went back to bed. "When I sat down on the bed, I became my sick self again who could barely lean over the bowl to steam my head clear...."

This all seems terribly primitive to my "enlightened" intellect, but I must reconcile myself to the fact that I do indeed believe in miracles. And I am willing to be an agent of such healing grace, now that I have experienced it firsthand. Why is such a phenomenon so incredible to us? Our traditions are founded upon such supernatural occurrences, and they speak to us of a universe where these occurrences are not the exception, but the norm.

When in Paul's epistle he exhorts us to "bear each other's burdens" we should perhaps take him more literally. It is natural for us to exhibit compassion—"suffering with"—towards one another, and to accept such kindness and communion. We may be the instruments of grace and profound healing to one another. The witness of our tradition and the wisdom of so many of our sister faiths speak this to us, that we may indeed "bear each other's burdens." There is a world around us groaning with the weight.

Ritual: Religion in Action

I used to think that ritual was evil. I had an evangelical upbringing in which "ritual" was the second half of the longer word "emptyritual," which sums up most evangelical attitudes towards ceremony as a means of worship. I learned that the "emptyritual" of Catholics was demonic and there was to be no evidence of symbols or ceremony in genuine, Godly religion. Thus, worship was solely an intellectual exercise. The body, which was repugnant to God because of our sin, could never be used as an instrument of praise (the vocal chords were okay, though). It was in college that I began to note the fallacies of world-hating theologies. I had seen too much, I suppose. I had noticed God in the majesty of the wild, in the cathedrals of caverns, in the ecstasy of passion, and in the eyes of even my "infidel" friends. The God of my experience burst through the boundaries of my childhood theology and demanded to be expressed. It was through a bit of synchronicity, or as Charles Williams calls it, "holy luck," that I discovered the glory of Catholic worship. I could barely contain my exhilaration as, for the first time in my life, I engaged the mystery of the Universe with the fullness of my being. I understood, as Evelyn Underhill states in her classic *Worship*, that rituals are "therefore more, not less valid expressions of the Spirit of Worship, because they belong at one and the same time to the world of sense and the world of spirit: for this is the actual situation of the amphibious creature by whom these means have been devised and used." "I am not a disembodied brain!" I rejoiced, and, in crossing myself, kneeling, singing, smelling the smoke of incense, and tasting of the Eucharist, I began to discover the holiness of myself and my world at every possible opportunity. A Mass junkie was born.

This was the beginning of my love affair with ritual. As I started to explore ritual outside of the Christian tradition, I discovered it to be an integral part of the religious life of nearly all peoples in every time. Ritual is the norm of human religious expression, it was my upbringing that was the anomaly. In discovering ritual's power, I not only found myself at one with the historical church, but also with the whole of humankind throughout history.

What Ritual Is

Victor Turner, in his book *The Ritual Process*, describes ritual as "a stereotyped sequence of activities involving gestures, words, and objects, performed in a sequestered place and designed to influence preternatural entities or forces on behalf of the actor's goals and interests." This description—the best I could find—is inadequate. Though it does describe the actual action, such a definition cannot hope to convey its essence. To quote Underhill again, ritual provides worshippers with "something to do, and also incites them to do it...exhibiting its kinship with the dance. For, as we must abandon ourselves to the dance, lose ourselves in it, in order to dance well, and 'learn by dancing that which is done;' so too with the religious rite. We can never understand it without taking part in it; moving with its movement, and yielding to its suggestions." It is more than movement and words, it is spirit in action, it is art. Turner's definition hints at this by calling the participants "actors," for that is exactly what they are. Ritual is sacred drama, and as such, if the performance is good, this art, like music or painting or dance, can capture our imaginations and emotions, and have the opportunity to transform us. In ritual we may create a thing of great beauty in collaboration with the Spirit, that may nourish all that it touches.

What Ritual Does

Ritual is a method for relating to universal Mystery and the mysteries of our personal lives. With it we are able to create boundaries within which we can order our world. Setting aside sacred space is an example of this. By ritually identifying an area as special, holy, we can contemplate the meaning of holy ground; get to know it, learn how to step in it. Then, when we think of all of the Earth as sacred ground, it means something to us. We know what holy ground is, we've felt it, and we can enter it with our full appreciation and wonder.

The same is true of sacred time. Time that is identified as sacred time cannot be described or measured by linear, chronological means, nor, indeed, any means at all. Ritual provides us access to Kairos, the Dreamtime, God's time. Time as God perceives it is at once instantaneous and eternal, since the Creator of Time must by necessity reside outside of it as well as inside. Speaking figuratively, for God to look to the left would be to behold the Creation, the parting of the Red Sea and the Crucifixion; to look to the right God would see what is future to us now, even to the end of the worlds and beyond. All time exists at once, and when we enter Kairos, all times are directly accessible to us.

For the Jewish faithful, the Seder does not recall to the memories of the participants an event several thousand years ago, but instead transports them to the event itself. In eating the bitter herbs, they don't merely remember the pain of their ancestors, they participate in their suffering. Drinking the wine doesn't help them remember the joy of their salvation from the pharaoh, it celebrates and communicates that joy and that salvation.

Similarly, when I, as a Christian, celebrate the Eucharist, it is not as an isolated event taking place on Sunday morning or Thursday afternoon, but an event out of linear time when I return via the ritual to the actual moment of Christ's crucifixion, witnessing God's sacrifice not alone, but in the company of all who have engaged in this ritual through the long corridors of history. The ritual provides for us a way to turn history into experience.

How Ritual Works

Ritual admits us in our conscious state to what we are used to engaging only when we are dreaming: the world of symbol, of archetype. As a child in church, I was told that we couldn't worship the Eucharist like the heathen Catholics did. The elements, were, after all, "just symbols," as if symbols were of little account.

If only I had known then what I know now about the power possessed by "just symbols." These "just symbols" are "the point where physical and metaphysical meet—a half-way house, where the world of things and the world of Spirit unite, and produce a new thing possessed of sensible and supra-sensible reality. And [people, who partake] of this double character, find in it the natural means of access to God" (Underhill).

Also, like dreams, the symbol in ritual is not easily exhausted. It brings to us many gifts, for it is multi-vocal, speaking to us a chorus of meanings; much more than we are ever prepared to hear. It whispers to our psyche dark secrets from the collective unconscious which we can never fully know.

Rupert Sheldrake, author of *The Rebirth of Nature*, has also proffered the theory of morphic resonance, "the idea that similar patterns of activity do indeed resonate through time," and therefore, "rituals may be doing just what people think they're doing —reconnecting, bringing the past into the present. And they may be reconnecting the present performance of the ritual not only with the original one, but with all the people who have done it over the preceding years." The implication of this is that every time a ritual is performed, its power is reinforced in the collective unconscious, increasing the vitality of its active archetypes.

Another theory is that offered by the rediscovered Huna, the shamanic tradition of Hawaii. According to Huna, the person is a composite of three distinct consciousnesses: the lower self, or physical, animal nature, incorporating our instinctive and intuitive nature; the middle self, or the rational, thinking, and responsible nature; and the higher self, which is our spiritual, ultimate nature. This is not an unfamiliar model, but Huna's unique insight is that the middle self and the higher self are strictly incommunicado. The rational self's only means of communication with the higher self is through the assistance of the lower self. The higher self will only recognize information in the form of embodied symbolism. Richard Smoley, editor of *Gnosis*, comments that "the success of a [Huna] ritual, in fact, depends entirely on how well it involves the lower self." The body and mind must work together if the whole self, body, mind, and spirit are to live in communion.

The Promise (and Danger) of Ritual

Ritual deserves our attention and respect, especially in the present times, when so much of what we treasure is threatened due to our greed and apathy. It has been said that nothing has power unless we give it. This is true of both the spirit of despair that hangs over our peoples and of the spiritual traditions we have neglected. Ritual can, like anything else in Creation, be abused. It can be used for selfish or destructive ends. It can indeed be "emptyritual," rendered impotent and boring by a poor performance. But like all art, like music and poetry, one only gets as much out as one puts in. True art is hard work, it can't be tossed off or immediately comprehended in all its complexity. Ritual isn't meant to entertain, it is a tool for us to work with, and whether we are the dancing shaman or the busy parishioner, we might as well stay home if we can't put forth the effort required to engage this mystery ourselves. Fortunately, one of the elements of great art is that when we are too exhausted or indifferent to give it our all, it is still powerful enough to touch us, to communicate its grace, to pick us up and carry us. This is especially true of the Mass, being a performance piece finely tuned for nearly two millennia.

Another danger is that of perspective. What does the rite communicate for us? To quote Underhill again, "Ritualism represents the constant tendency of the human creature to attach absolute value to his [or her] own activities." Our Christian rites have for too long viewed the Mass as the center of Christianity, Christianity as the center of humanity, and humanity as the center of Creation. Fortunately we know today that we live in a much larger universe, and our rites must evolve, through either form or interpretation (and most likely both), if they are to aid our growth rather than hinder it. Murray Hope relates an old Buddhist story "about a man who went searching for God beneath a stone, but in the process of lifting the stone he became so absorbed with its quality and beauty that he forgot his initial reason for raising it."[1] Valid ritual for us today will serve to eliminate walls between peoples and cultures rather than building them; they will communicate to us our proper place in the cosmos, our kinship to the Earth and our citizenship of and solidarity with the universe.

Hsün Tzu describes the Confucian view of what ritual should accomplish: "When rites are at their best, people's emotions and sense of beauty are both fully expressed.... It is through rites that heaven and earth are harmonious and sun and moon are bright, that the four seasons are ordered and the stars are on their courses, that rivers flow and that things prosper, that love and hatred are tempered and joy and anger are in keeping.... He who holds to the rites is never confused in the midst of multifarious change."

Anthony Wallace says that ritual "is the primary phenomenon of religion.... Ritual is religion in action; it is the cutting edge of the tool. Belief, although its recitation may be a part of the ritual, or a ritual in its own right, serves to explain, to rationalize, to interpret and direct the energy of the ritual performance...[but] it is ritual which accomplishes what religion sets out to do." Rituals must speak to us the truth about who we are. They must awaken us to the larger realities to which our limited sensibilities are blind. They must be enacted because we are embodied creatures who should not divorce our flesh from our spirit. They must be celebrated because we have so much, even from day to day, to celebrate.

NOTE

1   Hope, Murray. *Psychology of Ritual* (Rockport, MA: Element Books, 1991).

Who Do You Trust?

The Issue of Spiritual Authority

A few weeks ago I was attending a pagan seasonal festival with another former Southern Baptist, and found myself commiserating with her over the final death of the "Baptist ideal." As wine flowed, fire crackled, and our pagan friends danced with abandon, my friend and I, both liberal Christian clergy, were discussing the recent affair of a North Carolina Southern Baptist Church which had decided to bless homosexual unions.

The decision, as we heard the story, had come with no small amount of prayer and consideration. When their board of deacons decided in favor of the unions, all hell broke loose in the Convention.

This is hardly surprising. We had been watching with increasing uneasiness as the denomination slowly became more and more reactionary and fundamentalist. The fundamentalist takeover is by now pretty much complete, with Southern Baptist moderates forming their own sub-denominational groups.

Finally it was decided that this particular church should be expelled from the Convention. This is a historic decision, because one of the things that makes Baptists Baptist is the hardcore belief in the autonomy of the local church.

Early Baptist history is really quite rebellious and anything but authoritarian. Classically, the individual church decides what it will and will not do and teach. Pastors have the pulpit, but it is up to the deacons (laity all, the equivalent of elders or the vestry) to hire, fire, and make the "big" decisions.

But then, my friend—who had actually studied Baptist history in depth—told me of a doctrine which lies at the very foundation of Baptist thought, but which neither of us had ever heard in all of our years growing up in the denomination: the doctrine of "soul competency."

Mostly a reaction against authoritarian clericalism in the Roman and Reformed churches, "soul competency" proclaimed the right of each individual believer to decide for him or herself how they interpret the scriptures.

This radical idea gives one a glimpse of just how revolutionary the early Baptists were, and how far removed those who currently use that name are from their predecessors. To quote the Psalmist: "O how the mighty are fallen."

Similarly, few of my Roman Catholic friends are aware of the declaration of "internal authority" found in the *Declaration on Religious Freedom* of the Vatican II documents. "Internal authority" refers to the individual's responsibility to follow his or her conscience regardless of whether that conscience is in conflict with civil or religious authorities. I personally know many faithful Roman Catholic people who exercise artificial birth control, yet agonize over what is, after all, common sense and good conscience.

Why the secrecy? Why is it a secret that the final religious authority resides *within* each one of us, *for* each one of us? Why do we hand over our power so quickly, so willingly?

Because we were taught to do so. In their phenomenal book on religious authoritarianism, *The Guru Papers*, Joel Kramer and Diana Alstad write that "if children are taught to mistrust themselves...as adults they will have little option other than looking for someone else to trust." They go on to explain that if people are conditioned not to trust themselves, "they will give away what power they have to those they think can protect them. The problem is that in doing so, *one is no longer protected from one's protec-tors....* This leads to corrupt, power-driven hierarchies that care little about the well-being of people" (emphasis mine).

Although hierarchical abuse is no stranger to Buddhism, the Buddha claimed no divine inspiration or external authority. His teaching condemns "blind faith," and emphasizes trust in one's own personal experience and capacity for critical judgment. "Be not led by the authority of religious texts," the Buddha said, "nor by mere logic or inference...nor by the idea 'this is our teacher.' But...*when you know for yourselves* that certain things are whole-some and good, then accept them and follow them."

The Goddess tradition, too, is exemplary in advocating oneself as prime spiritual authority. Ginia Webster in the *Temenos Journal* says that self-trust in regard to spiritual matters is crucial to liv-ing the "Goddess Lifestyle." "It is," she says, "following your inner voice instead of listening to external pressures. It is trusting your own wisdom, and knowing that the details will fall into place as you move in the direction of your heart's path. It is trusting with confidence that you know what you know, you see what you see, you feel what you feel."

It is like my pagan friends in ecstatic motion all around us, trusting their hearts, trusting their feet. And now I wonder to myself, why is it that my friend and I were mourning on the bench, instead of dancing in the Spirit?

Magic: Mysticism or Manipulation?

What are we to make of magic? We use this same word to describe the date that went well, slight of hand entertainment, and the arcane manipulation of metaphysical forces. We are attracted to it for its mystery, and yet afraid of it because of our cultural conditioning.

As a new student at the Institute in Culture and Creation Spirituality in Oakland, California a few years ago, I found myself—a cradle Evangelical and current Episcopalian—in Starhawk's class on Native European Ritual. Now, as far as I was concerned at the time, Native European Ritual was a euphemism for nothing less than witchcraft, and I found it to be quite a challenge learning to adjust, psychologically. Was what I was doing wrong? Is there any possibility that the anti-witchcraft fundamentalist protesters at Matthew Fox's lectures might actually be right? Was I going to hell for "acing" my Ritual class? In the beginning, this was a persistent nagging that wouldn't leave me alone. But I have had plenty of time since then to process, research, and actually get to know several "pagans" personally.

What I have discovered is that there are two primary motivations for ritual magic: mysticism and manipulation. Mysticism is the enjoyment of, or pursuit after, the experience of union with the Divine, and many magical rituals do indeed earnestly seek this goal.

With mysticism, one seeks the experience of oneness with all that is, to pierce the illusion of seeming dualism so embraced by our culture to recognize oneself as one is, a small part of a much larger whole.

It seems to me that, although many pagans speak of such concepts as "oneness" and pantheism, many rituals attempt to impose one's will upon another element of Creation, be it the weather, the outcome of something anticipated, or, more dangerously, another animal or human being. The conflict here is that the imposition of one's will upon another—manipulation—denies oneness and reinforces the appearance of duality. In this instance magic is employed to gain "power-over," in order to control another.

Mysticism or manipulation. Magic can serve either purpose.

For the mystically-oriented magician, the practice involves the process of "emptying." This is very like Taoism, which is not surprising: it, like Wicca, is a Native tradition. In the *Tao Te Ching* (the principal scripture of Taoism) Lao Tzu writes, "If you can empty yourself of everything, you will have lasting peace.... If you want to be filled, become empty." In emptying we let go of our own desires; the ego is transcended and with it all thought of personal gain or power. We surrender in this act our need to control to that Oneness that we cannot hope to comprehend or control. When we are able to do this, we exchange "power-over" for "power-with," for we have the wise will of the Universe working for us.

The Taoist sage knows that it is useless to resist the flow of the Tao, "One who relies on the Tao," writes Lao Tzu, "Does not enforce his will...for such things are likely to rebound."

When we do not trust the Tao, we try to manipulate our environment in order to artificially influence the flow of events. This can take the familiar and mundane form of bribery or physical threats, while in more esoteric efforts, the Earth's energies can be so directed as to achieve what one wills. What is dangerous about this is not only the danger of abusing that which is acted upon, but the presumption of the practitioner that they know what is best for the situation. What lunacy! No one can hope to know the scope of the Tao, or the outcome of the present flow of events. "The Tao will always be beyond comprehension," Lao Tzu says, for "although it may seem trivial, no one in all the world can control it."

The pagans I know are of the mystic variety, and are exceedingly scrupulous about their magical designs. A common bumper sticker seen these days in the Bay Area is one that reads "Witches Heal." Healing, whether for a person, an animal, or the Earth herself is indeed, in my experience, the end towards which most magical work is directed. Witches in this tradition believe in what they call the "Three-fold Return," which holds that any harm one intends another through magical work will be visited upon the sender three-fold. A compelling law, indeed. Most pagans also subscribe to some form of the law of Karma, familiar from Eastern traditions, which guarantees that impartial justice is operative in the universe. Lao Tzu says "Heaven's Way is to nourish, not to harm. The Sage's Way is to work, yet not compete."

To return to our opening question—"What are we to make of magic?"—we do magic a gross injustice to label it "evil," as so many in our culture have been eager to do. Pagans are no more likely than practitioners of any faith tradition to have nefarious ends in mind. Magic is not evil. What is evil is the attempt to force the hand of the Divine, to contest against the flow of the Tao, the will to control what we cannot even hope to comprehend. And this applies as much to a member of the Order of the Golden Dawn as it does to the pastor of the Holiness Baptist Church down the block. According to the *Tao Te Ching*, the wise practitioner "unlearns what she was once taught, and helps the people regain what they have lost, to help every being assume its natural state, and not dare to force anything."

Each in their Own Tongues

It is in Genesis that we read about the hubris of those who dared think they could build a tower big enough to touch God. "Here they are," says the Lord, "one people with a single language...henceforth nothing they have a mind to do will be beyond their reach.... Let us go down there and confuse their speech, so that they will not understand what they say to one another" (New English Bible).

We are used to thinking of this passage as being a parallel to its neighbor story in Genesis, the Flood. They are stories of punishment and wrath. If, however, we sever this story from the first, it does not necessarily speak ill of these people, but only reveals God's persistent penchant for diversity. We need only look to the world of Nature to see that the animals are wildly diverse in their colors, shapes, and, more so even than we, in the multiplicity of their speech.

The Tower of Babel is not an icon on which to hang the blame for humanity's chaos and division, but the mythic starting point of the planet's varied cultures. After the flood, the myth goes, there was only Noah's family with which to repopulate the world. After a few generations, these many people, it makes sense to say, would speak the same language and be from the same culture, that which survived the flood on the ark. But Babel is the second creation of the human race, where we each have gone our own way and blossomed forth our uniquenesses wherever we found suitable space to flourish.

In Hinduism, we find that the diversity of the universe exists only as an illusion. All of Creation is a huge, spiraling dance of the Creator God of whom all things are members. The purpose of the universe for the Hindu is for all the fragmented and apparently separate "selves" to wake up and recognize their true identity: God. This is the joy of existence, for God to recognize Godself in perpetuity.

Likewise, in the myth of the Tower of Babel, the single body of humankind is disguised in the going forth and development of distinct cultures. The goal of our existence in a new and glorious global home is to wake up and recognize each other as a part of our whole—and united—humanity.

The conclusion of the story of the Tower of Babel is found, I believe, in the account of the coming of the Holy Spirit at Pentecost. In this New Testament myth, scripture says "suddenly there came from the sky a noise like that of a strong driving wind, which filled the whole house...and there appeared to them tongues like flames of fire, dispersed among them and resting on each one. And they were all filled with the Holy Spirit and began to talk in other tongues, as the Spirit gave them power of utterance." This is a frightening and confusing scene, and we can only speculate what is meant in this passage by "tongues." But further on, at least, it is clear that "there were living in Jerusalem devout men and women drawn from every nation under heaven; and at this sound the crowd gathered, all bewildered because each one heard in their own tongue."

In this scene we have a great truth of the universe embedded in mythology. But because it is our mythology, we are often reluctant to dig it out and explore it. Like other great events in scripture, it speaks to us not as an isolated event that happened only at one point in history. Though it very well may have had a historical basis in fact, it is more important to us for what truth it can tell us about our experience as a body of humanity now and throughout all time.

It tells us that the Holy Spirit does not rest upon one head, but upon all that are present. It tells us that the Holy Spirit is familiar with the speech and cultures of all of God's peoples. And not only is this an affirmation of our diversity, but the text says that each of those present heard what was said in their own tongues. The Holy Spirit is polylingual—she does not speak only Aramaic or Greek or Jacobean English. For how could it possibly be that the Spirit of God would abandon any peoples at any time, anywhere?

"Each heard in their own tongue." This tells us that God is not the exclusive property of the Jews or the Christians. All throughout history, the Holy Spirit has whispered, "and each one heard in their own tongue," their own language, their own symbols, their own culture. When the people of Babel scattered to the four corners of the Earth, none went alone. For the Spirit of God who constantly cares for us, who nourishes our spirits, and breathes life into the wombs of every people alike, was their light and their salvation.

One doesn't have to study the religions of the world for very long before it becomes obvious that the God who peers out at me from the tortured brow of the crucifix is the same being who winks mischievously from the betrunked figure of the Hindu god Ganesh. This eye makes contact with my own, and I recognize in that gleam the loving greeting of my Beloved.

When the Lord in the Gospel of St. Matthew tells us to go into every nation and proclaim the Gospel, we need to remember that this was the command of God all along to the Jews, Matthew's intended audience. The Gospel, or Good News, is the revelation of God as the Healer, the Redeemer, the Lover, and the Bearer of Justice, whose faces we can recognize in every conceivable culture's art, and indeed, in every people's tongues.

A Companion on the Journey

Interfaith Spiritual Direction

Fifteen hundred years ago, a Buddhist monk named Bodhidharma traveled to China at the invitation of the emperor. This emperor was very proud of his support of Buddhism in his country, and wanted to know how much merit he had accrued for his efforts. When Bodhidharma finally presented himself, the emperor lost no time in asking, "So how much merit have I accrued?"

"None to speak of," said Bodhidharma with a yawn.

"What?" the Emperor wailed. This did not square with what his local teacher had told him, which was that you get as good as you give, so he was stymied and didn't know what to think. In fact, this didn't sound like any Buddhism *he* knew of. "Well, then what is the meaning of Buddhism?" he asked.

Bodhidharma picked his teeth with a splinter and replied without looking up, "Vast emptiness and no meaning whatsoever."

The emperor's jaw dropped. He simply did not know what to think. "Who *are* you?" He asked the monk.

"I have no idea," Bodhidharma smiled up at him.

This is good spiritual direction. A lot of people want spiritual direction, but they do not know that such a ministry even exists. And when they find it, they often find, like the emperor above, that it does not provide easy answers as they had hoped. Instead, it focuses us on the difficult questions our lives present to us, and helps us to make careful and soulful discernments, supported by a sympathetic companion.

"Spiritual direction" is really a horrible description of this ministry, and yet, due to history, that is the name that most people recognize. Like Bodhidharma when he first met the emperor, spiritual guides do not actually do much "directing." We don't tell people what to think, or what to believe, or how they are supposed to feel, or what to do in any specific circumstance. Mostly we just sit there. Like Bodhidharma, we may even pick our teeth on occasion.

This is good practice. Because what most people need is not another person—who is allegedly an "expert"—to tell them what to think or do or how to behave. There are enough spiritual busybodies around who will gladly oblige if that is what you want, and they will do it for free. A real spiritual director, though, listens carefully to what you have to say, asks a lot of questions, and points out things he or she notices that you may have missed. A real spiritual director believes that the person who comes for direction is the expert on his or her spiritual life, and deep down, knows what is best. It's that "deep down" wisdom that a spiritual director is good at helping people uncover.

There are lots of kinds of spiritual directors. Some work with people of specific religions, usually their own. This makes sense: a Buddhist spiritual director will be able to be very helpful to a seeker who is also a Buddhist. But a lot of spiritual directors are not tradition-specific in this way and often call themselves "interfaith." An interfaith spiritual director does not care what religion you are, or even if you have a religion. Religion is really not always that important. An interfaith spiritual director will help you discern what your spiritual path is, and will encourage you to walk it to the best of your ability—even if it is weird, even if it is very different from his or her own path. Interfaith spiritual directors are not afraid of people whose spirituality is different from theirs, because they know that they have just as much to learn from the spiritual direction encounter as the person seeking direction.

If you have never been to spiritual direction, it kind of looks like psychotherapy, at least from the outside. Two people sit in a room in chairs that face each other, and talk for about an hour. But this is where the similarities to therapy end. While in therapy you might discuss your emotional life or perhaps why you hate your mother, the content of the spiritual direction session is usually very specific and focused on the seeker's spiritual life.

You might still talk about why you hate your mother, but your spiritual guide will patiently wait for you to finish, and will then probably ask you how holding on to those feelings affects your feelings of connection to the Divine. If you picture divinity as Mother Earth, you can see how this could be very significant indeed.

Interfaith spiritual direction is non-dogmatic and non-coercive. This doesn't mean that interfaith spiritual directors are pushovers, though. Like the emperor, people often have a difficult time with things their spiritual director has to say. This is because we in the West have usually been told that if you do A, B, and C, in the right order and without asking any inconvenient questions, your spiritual life will be dandy.

This is, of course, crap. The spiritual journey is the most difficult thing most of us will ever endeavor to do. It means that the person we thought we were often has to die so that the person we really are can show up. It means that we sometimes have to let go of cherished notions that no longer serve us, and that can be as difficult as prying Linus' blanket out of his fingers. And we usually don't have to do these things once, but over and over. It's excruciating, it's exhausting. And there's no road map to show us exactly how to get from here to there—no instruction manual to tell us the "right" way to do it.

Fortunately, we don't have to do it alone. That's where spiritual direction comes in. A spiritual director will walk with you on your spiritual journey, will listen as you uncover your true purpose, and will support you as you discover your true path. He or she will point out things that you may be too close to see, but you don't have to take their word for anything. You are *always* the expert on your spiritual life.

You can also trust your spiritual director to be truthful. Like Bodhidharma, when the emperor asked him how much merit he had earned, your spiritual director will not tell you only those things you want to hear. When he or she hears a load of crap, he or she is going to say, "Sounds like a load of crap." This is good direction, and a wise person will value the opinion, even if he or she does not share it.

For many of us, spiritual direction is an essential part of our journeys. Just as you wouldn't set off across the desert alone, it helps to have a soul friend along for the journey, because when your canteen is empty, it's a good bet your director's is not.

That is why the school I teach at requires their students to have a spiritual director. It is a deep spiritual program, and lots of "stuff" emerges while people are going through it. Having a spiritual director to talk to while you are sorting through all this "stuff" is very helpful indeed.

Like Bodhidharma, spiritual directors do not have the answers, and the good ones don't pretend to. But we do have a warm, hospitable space to offer, a cup of tea to share, and our full attention to give. It is not certainty we offer, but presence, because no one needs to walk the spiritual path alone.

Krishna: Lover of Our Souls

Krishna had a thing for cowgirls. It's true! In the literature of the epic period of Hindu history we find numerous stories about the Lord Krishna and his exploits with, well, cowgirls. The cowgirls in this literature are called the gopis, and they quite clearly had a thing for Krishna, too.

One night Krishna decided to go dancing with the gopis, so after midnight, he took his flute and went out into the woods and began to play.

You've heard of the pied piper? Can't hold a candle to Krishna! The cowgirls went bonkers. They flew out of bed, made hasty excuses to their parents or their husbands and took off for the forest.

Now, when the gopis found Krishna, like the playful lover he is, he teased them, saying, "My goodness! How nice of you all to drop in on me like this! But really, it's a little late, and you should be in bed." This only made them laugh, because Krishna has never been one for following the rules or being discreet.

So then Krishna said, "The forest is a dangerous place with animals like tigers, bears, jackals, and wolves. Your families must be worried about you. You should hurry back home at once." This of course also made them laugh because they were in the presence of the supreme identity of the Godhead and they weren't the least bit worried about tigers.

Krishna kept teasing them and trying to get them to go home, and they finally got a little miffed at him and told him not to be so mean.

They said, "Krishna, we love you so much and you promised us we would have you as our husband." So then Krishna kissed them all and they started to romp through the forest, singing and dancing.

And then suddenly, Krishna was gone! He just disappeared.

The gopis were dismayed and started to look everywhere for him. They broke out the flashlights and organized a search. But you know, when Krishna wants to hide....

Finally they gave up and just started to play. Then they started to play like they were Krishna! One of them pretended to be the demon Putana, and another became Krishna taking her milk. One gopi became a handcart and another kicked her legs as Krishna did in another myth to break the cart. One gopi played on a flute. They had a wonderful, wonderful time.

Then they got tired and they sat down and started chanting that "Hare Krishna" chant—it's very old!—and then suddenly... there he was, standing before them! Lord Krishna suddenly came out of hiding. The gopis made a seat for him in the sand and put nice cloth over it. Sitting on the seat with the gopis, Krishna became even more beautiful. He said, "Sometimes I hide from you, but do not think I was away from you. I was very near and watching you. Please don't be disturbed. Just be happy." And so Krishna began to dance hand in hand with the gopis. He put his hands on the shoulders of each gopi on both sides of him. He danced with every one of them, though each one thought only she was dancing with Krishna.

(Now a lot of people think that the Rasa Dance, as this story is called, doesn't have anything to do with dancing, but with love-making, which really isn't all that different, really. And since each of the cowgirls felt like they had married Krishna that night, there might be something to that.)

After the Rasa Dance finished, just an hour or two before sunrise, Krishna said, "It is time to leave." They did not want to go, but they did. And they were all ecstatic, because for one unbelievable night, they had each been Krishna's lover.

This is a wonderful story, and it obviously has a lot to say to us as human beings or it wouldn't have been around so long. What does this dancing figure of Krishna mean for us? Why does he delight us? Why does he provoke us? Why does he make *us* want to dance?

I can't give any kind of definitive answer to these questions, but I can offer some suggestions. Mechtild of Magdeburg, a medieval Christian mystic, once said, "The day of my spiritual awakening was the day I saw—and knew I saw—all things in God, and God in all things." Now when she said this, she wasn't just talking about forests and streams; she was also talking about human beings. We are as much a part of the Divine as the foam on the waves and the songs of birds.

When the gopis started to reenact the stories they knew of Krishna, they made him present in their midst. They were, in a sense, having church, playing out the roles of their myths with their own bodies and imaginations, making them new and real, something that truly belonged to *them*. They became Krishna for each other, and their play continued.

Meister Eckhardt says that we are all to be Mary; that we are all to give birth to Christ in our own time, in ourselves, in our community. Therefore, all of Creation is what is called in theological terms a "theophany," the incarnation of God, and we are all *avatars*, the incarnations of God on Earth. The *Tao Te Ching* says that "the Tao unites with all of dust," and when I receive ashes on Ash Wednesday I am reminded that I am that dust. So are you.

When Evangelical writer Tony Campolo said that he saw Jesus in every person he met, he was put on trial for heresy. I say, "Cheers!" to you, Tony Campolo. You are in better company with the heretics.

Let us join Tony Campolo in believing Jesus when he said, "What you do to the least of these you do to me." God is in us as assuredly as God ever was in Jesus of Nazareth, or in Krishna the cow-herder, or any of the other traditional forms in which we hear the truth spoken. And the truth is this: that God has come to Earth, and is walking among us.

Why is this important to us? I think we have had enough of the old-white-male-in-the-sky kind of God. We don't need a God who is away out there, is keeping a tally of our mistakes and is going to get us when we die. Such a notion is *not* conducive to an attitude of trust to people in our society. We no longer relate to the idea of a King sitting on a throne as the head of our government, trusting that he has our "best interests" in mind.

We have evolved into a democracy, where the power is held in the hands of the people, and we now long not for a God of power and might, but one of immediacy and intimacy. We want a God who with cry with us and hold us to her breast, not one who rides out of the sky on a white horse to conquer our enemies. We want intimacy, want warmth, and most of all, we want *humanity*.

The stories of Jesus are testament to this intuition: we need a God who bleeds, cries, and dies. We need a God who understands our pain and our fears. The stories of Krishna tell of a God full of sensuality, who loves music, and lovemaking, and play. These are Gods we can use, Gods that make sense to us, because they speak to the heart of what it means to be human.

The Jungian psychologist Robert A. Johnson wrote about a journey to India. He said, "A friend took me to Calcutta, the darkest city of India, dedicated to Kali, the goddess of destruction, the most horrific of the goddesses. My friend left me there for three days alone while he went to visit his parents in a section of India forbidden to foreigners. I was not afraid of India by that time but I had not reckoned on the terrors of Calcutta. Soon my courage was eroded away and I could not stand one more amputated arm thrust into my ribs or another corpse to step over on the street. The final straw was a woman who thrust a dead baby into my arms in hopes that I could restore it to life for her. I have rarely been totally defeated in my life but this was such an event.

"I started to go to pieces, and it was the only time in India I have ever been overwhelmed by the darkness of it. In my anguish all I needed was somebody—somebody to be close to, somebody to hear me, somebody to talk to. I know what to do.... It is a custom in India that you can go to another person—anyone, man or woman, young or old, stranger on the street, trusted friend, any-one—and ask that person if he or she will be the incarnation of God for you.... So I went off to the park, began looking around, chose a middle-aged Indian of serene face, dressed in traditional Indian clothing, and went up to him.

"The first question was, 'Do you speak English?' 'Yes.' Second question, 'Will you be the incarnation of God for me?' He looked me straight in the eye—rare—and said, 'Yes.' So for twenty min-utes the dam broke and I poured out my fright and my misery and my loneliness, and the anguish of three days of Calcutta which had been accumulating in me. I felt better. I just needed somebody, some human being to parallel or to understand or to walk with me for a minute, and bear this anguish of an intensity that I'd never known before."

We must all be the incarnation of God for each other. We must incarnate the lover of our souls by comforting one another, by feeding one another, by supporting and understanding one another. Therese of Lisieux once said, "Jesus has no hands on Earth but yours." Jesus has no hands on Earth but *yours*.

Therefore, I say to you, welcome, my God and savior. As we see God in the stars, in the pageantry of the forest, let us also see Divinity in one another.

If you will close your eyes, and center yourself, I invite you to call up an image: not of an angry father or a scolding teacher, but of your dearest and most trusted friend. In your mind's eye, go to them and embrace them, and ask them to be the incarnation of God for you. They say yes. Now, what would you like to say to God? Say it. This is your friend. The one that loves you com-pletely, the one that understands. Say what you have been need-ing to say all of your life....

Now return to the room, bringing your incarnation of God with you. (Wow! It's suddenly pretty crowded in here!)

Robert Johnson's story has an ending. After he poured his heart out to this man, he said, "[The man] helped just by listening. He was the incarnation of God for me. I thanked him and told him that I had recovered my manners and was sorry about this out-burst.

"I said, 'And now please tell me who you are.' He gave me his name, which was unrememberable, and said, quite simply, 'I am a [Catholic] priest.'

"Now, there are very few Christians in India, and certainly very, very few priests. And of all the people in Calcutta I could have asked to be the incarnation of God for me," he says, "I had picked out a Roman Catholic priest! I was just astonished. He took me by the hand, got lunch for me, paid for it before I could function, bade me good-bye, and walked off."

Proving, of course, that God comes to us in the most unlikely people. Why not in you?

A Matter of Perspective

When I was in fifth grade, I had a teacher named Mr. Mobley. Mr. Mobley was as tall as Lurch in the Addams Family TV show, and just as lovable beneath his gruff exterior. One day he was reading an assignment I had written while he hovered above my desk. He put his hand on top of my head and playfully examined my skull with his fingers while he read. I was enjoying this rare display of affection, until his fingers were suddenly arrested in their exploration. At the rear of the top of my head, on either side were two pronounced knots. Once his fingers found them, they distracted his attention from the paper he was holding, and he spent the next several moments examining my head with great interest. Finally, he looked at me like I was from Mars and announced, "You're going to sprout horns, soon."

I panicked and felt at the top of my head. Sure enough, two little raised knots were back there, and every day for weeks I checked to make sure the pointy tips of horns had not yet broken through the skin.

Frightened as I was of being branded a biological freak, I was terrified of what horns might mean. Did it mean I was a devil? Did it mean I was going to hell? I told my best friend Mickey about it, and he offered helpfully, "Jews have horns, you know. That's why they wear those little beanies, so you can't see them."

"Wow!" I thought. Sure enough, one of those beanies would exactly cover up my emerging horns. But how could I be Jewish? I decided there was something my mother wasn't telling me.

I never asked my mother about this, mostly because we were devout Baptists, and I didn't know what it might mean if I were to be found out as a closet Jew. To this day my mother tells me that as a child I often told her I would become a Jew, but I never did confront her about my horns.

Now, in truth of course, it is much more likely that those knots were the result of being dropped on my head as an infant than indicators of some clandestine Semitic or demonic heritage, but to my fifth grade imagination, they posed quite a crisis of faith.

This notion that Jews have horns derives from a mistranslation of our first reading (Exodus 34) where Moses comes down from Mount Sinai. The Hebrew word translated "shining" is *qaran*. Other translators render this "rays of light," but in some early translations, the phrase was erroneously rendered "horns of light" or simply "horns." Now since they are both conically shaped you can see how "rays" and "horns" might be confused, especially since the same Hebrew word is used for both.

It is due to this mistranslation that the medieval tradition of Jews having horns came about. One little shift of meaning revealed the demonic—not in Jews, but in Christians, as it supported centuries of genocide and cruelty against the Jewish people. A tiny, one-word shift changed Moses from the hero of the story to a suspected devil in the minds of Christian readers.

In this case, a shift in meaning created a shift in perspective which brought about damnation—a hell on earth for Jews, and perhaps damnation proper for the Christians who persecuted them. But in many religions, just such a shift in perspective can also bring about salvation.

One of my favorite groups of early Christian heretics is the Gnostics, about whom you have heard me preach before. According to the Gnostics, this world is the creation of an inept and misguided demiurge, who suffers under the delusion that he is God, and wants us to believe it too, so that he can keep us captive on this prison planet, perpetually reincarnating and worshipping only him. The Gnostic insight is that he is not God at all, but only a pretender to the throne, and that the real God exists beyond the demiurge, and in fact, beyond our universe, where the fullness of the Godhead dwells in ineffable light. There is a spark of that true divinity in us, which seeks to be free of this earthly prison, and to rejoin the fullness of the Godhead.

This shift in perspective, from worshipping the creator to worshipping the true God beyond the material plane, constituted salvation for the Gnostics and freed their souls to fly beyond this world upon their deaths and to once again know communion with true Divinity.

Jung saw this story in less cosmic, more personal terms. In his transpersonal psychology, the goal of all spiritual practice is the recognition that, like the demiurge, our individual egos are simply pretenders to the throne. My ego, according to Jung, is not me. It does not begin to describe the fullness of who I am. For who I truly am exists within and yet beyond the confines of my body. According to Jung, and nearly every mystic in every religious tradition, there is but one great being in the universe, and that is who we really are. Call it God, call it the dynamic ground of all being, call it Brahma, the Body of Christ, or the Pleroma—there are many names, but there is only one person inhabiting the cosmos, and we are all limbs of that one great body.

And this realization is, for the mystics of all ages, salvation. When the Sufis were condemned because in their ecstasy they called out "I am Allah!" they were only stating the truth. Their perspective had shifted through their practice. They no longer fixed their identity to their individual egos, but experienced themselves as part of Allah himself. This body will die, but Allah cannot die. Flame burns, water drowns, old age withers, but Allah is touched by none of it. In this realization, the existential dread felt by all of us is lifted, because who we really are is infinite, immortal, and indestructible.

For this to happen, however, for this shift in perspective to really take hold, the ego's greatest fear—that it will someday die—must be realized. The ego must die to the idea that it is king, that it is in control, that it is immortal. The ego must step aside and allow the One who is truly immortal and infinite to occupy the throne of the heart. The ego's illusions of grandeur must die, and in that death, a new being can emerge.

This is symbolized in our own tradition by Jesus' determination to go to Jerusalem. He knows that the divine agenda can only be fulfilled if he dies, and so he sets his face towards the holy city, in spite of his disciples'—and no doubt, his own ego's—protestations. And what happens there? He is tried and condemned, and he is put to death. But what happens then? Only upon his death is the fullness of his divinity revealed. His resurrected body is indestructible, infinite, and immortal. Jesus' genius, according to Jung, was that he saw through the illusions of the ego, and found his identity in his Father, into whom he was eventually absorbed, even in our theology. "Very truly," Jesus tells us, "unless a grain of wheat falls into the earth and dies, it remains just a single grain; but if it dies, it bears much fruit."

In the Gospel of Thomas we are told that we are supposed to be Jesus' twin: to mirror him, to realize that the same shift in perspective he made can be made by us as well. We, too, are invited to see past the limitations of our own individual egos and embrace God as our true home, and indeed, our true identity.

This paschal mystery is played out not only in our personal journeys, but in our corporate life, as well. This little church, which identified itself so much with one fine tradition—the faith of the Pilgrim fathers—had first to die, in order to be resurrected as a community that embraces all faiths and honors the universal truths that defy all sectarian boundaries. We meet here today to celebrate this death and resurrection, and the truth that only after this transfiguration is embraced can we truly own our own lives, or in the case of our congregation, our own building. Jung calls this "individuation," Fr. Richard calls it "virginity," I call it "now that we know who we are, let us get on with the adventure of really living."

The problem with making this perceptual shift is that it inevitably comes at great personal cost. The church does not want to fold. The ego does not want to die. The disciples do not want Jesus to go to Jerusalem. The "old man," as Paul calls him, does not want to let go of his status, his identity, his life. The images attending this shift in our many mythologies are universally cataclysmic. For Hindus it is known as the *maha bharat,* the great war. For Muslems it is *jihad,* holy war. For Christians it is Armageddon. For you and me, however, we might just call it a spiritual emergency.

Even though it really takes place internally, the mythologies depict it as a great cosmic battle, and it feels cosmic indeed; it feels huge, it feels like the end of the world. And indeed, for the ego, it is.

But our traditions give us comfort, as well. For we do not go through this catastrophic shift alone. In the Hindu scripture, the *Bhagavad Gita,* Arjuna quails at the scene of the battle, but Krishna, the incarnate God, is with him to encourage him, and to assure him that since everyone is just a part of him, and he never dies, no one in reality dies, and nothing is ever lost. The disciples are comforted by Jesus, even as he marches toward death, as he assures them that "I and my father are one."

No divine comfort is sufficient to alleviate our anxiety, however. Until that great battle is fought, it is the scariest thing that we—or should I say our egos—will ever face. But we are promised that once the battle is fought, we will have victory, that on other side of the crucifixion is resurrection.

And this is another result of the shift in perspective: that which had previously been fierce becomes friendly. The God of terrible aspect, that so threatens our egos, becomes our loving Father who embraces us in love, and that which we most fear is transfigured into our surest hope.

Jung tells us that God, the great Self that embodies all of being, is constantly trying to break into our consciousness. This inbreaking always seems violent until we catch on and cooperate with the process. Through mythology, tradition, the unconscious, and dreams, the truth of who we really are is trying to impress itself upon us, if only we have ears to hear.

The Gospel of Thomas promises us that if we bring forth what is within us, what we bring forth will save us. But if we do not bring forth what is in us, what we fail to bring forth will destroy us. The ground of all Being is within us, whispering the truth of our divine origins to us at all times; as Revelation tells us, God stands at the door and knocks, seeking entrance to our conscious, waking life, and acknowledgment as the ground of our being. What will our answer be? Will we quail at the sight of the battle, or will we rouse ourselves to the charge? The fate of the universe may not hang in the balance, but the fate of our souls certainly may.

So, did the little knots on my head point to a satanic or sacred ancestry? Is Moses coming down from the mountain angelic or demonic? Is God a misguided demiurge or the source of infinite life and light? Is our end the grave or resurrection? It all depends upon your perspective.

Teilhard de Chardin and the Formation of the Noosphere

W hile he does not enjoy the visibility of many of the notable figures in transpersonal psychological circles, Teilhard de Chardin is undoubtedly one of the pioneers of the field. Even though he died more than a decade before transpersonal psychology, as such, even existed, yet his ideas, far-fetched though they sounded in his time, are undoubtedly well within the field. And, as we shall see, these ideas are beginning to seem less and less unlikely as time goes on.

Chardin was not a psychologist, nor even a philosopher in the usual sense. He was a priest and a paleontologist, to whom the concept of evolution held as much weight as scripture. "Evolution" is the basis for Chardin's entire cosmology. Not, as Darwinian evolution would have it, however, a random product, or the "survival of the fittest," but an evolution planned and guided by divine agency. "The magic word 'evolution' which haunted my thoughts like a tune," he writes, "was to me like unsatisfied hunger, like a promise held out to me, like a summons to be answered."[1] Chardin's universe is one of continuous and interwoven evolutionary threads, incorporating plants, animals, the planet, the cosmos, and, most peculiar to him, not merely the physical and mental evolution of humankind, but our spiritual ascent as well. Michael Murray writes,

> Man [is] at the growing tip of the evolutionary axis—man, the most complex and conscious entity so far produced by the universe as a whole. Physically small, but psychically the superlative result of all the synthetic labors of the stars, man is the spiritual, if not the spatial summit of the cosmos, the hope and instrument of its future consummation. Thus in Teilhard's hands the theory of evolution, far from diminishing man by relating him to the apes, as so many churchmen used to fear, actually re-establishes him at the moving apex of time-space, well above the fixed central position which he lost in the Copernican revolution.[2]

The evolutionary ascent of human beings occurs, according to Chardin's theory, in two stages of what he calls "planetization." The first stage is the "Go forth and multiply" stage, in which humanity expanded, in both quantity (in the very number of persons), and in quality (psychological and spiritual development). As Blanch Gallagher explains,

> During the long period of expansion, physical and cultural differences isolated the peoples of the Earth from each other as they spread to fill the Earth. At the beginning of our present century, with most of the habitable surface of the Earth occupied, the races began to converge. Through technology, tangential energy becomes evident in the response of the people across the Earth to each other; people are sharing their wars, their coronations, their concerns. Thus the law of complexity-consciousness develops.[3]

We have reached the end of the expanding, or "diversity" stage, and, are now entering the contracting, or "unifying" stage. At this point, Chardin's theory runs completely counter to Darwin's, in that the success of humanity's evolution in the second stage will not be determined by "survival of the fittest," but by our own capacity to converge and unify.[4] The most important initial evolutionary leap of the convergence stage is the formation of what Chardin termed "the Noosphere." Its formation, as Michael Murray explains, begins with

> ...a global network of trade, communications, accumulation and exchange of knowledge, cooperative research, mixture of populations and production of energy—all go into the weaving of the material support for a sphere of collective thought. In the field

of science alone, no individual knows more than a tiny fraction of the sum of scientific knowledge, and each scientist is dependent not only for his education but for all his subsequent work on the traditions and resources which are the collective possession of an entire international society composed of the living and the dead. Just as Earth once covered itself with a film of interdependent living organisms which we call the biosphere, so mankind's combined achievements are forming a global network of collective mind.[5]

"The idea," writes Chardin, "is that of the Earth not only covered by myriads of grains of thought, but enclosed in a single thinking envelope so as to form a single vast grain of thought on the sidereal scale, the plurality of individual reflections grouping themselves together and reinforcing one another in the act of a single unanimous reflection."[6] One hesitates to invoke the terms "group-mind" or "hive mentality," but they are perhaps, leaps made by far less developed creatures than we that presage our own ascent. We know that such a thing can and does exist in a variety of species, especially ants, migratory birds, and others. We also know the evidence regarding the "hundredth monkey" (once a learned behavior is taught to a significant portion of a population—in this famous example, of monkeys—the behavior becomes instinctual even for those completely isolated from the community which acquired the behavior). If C.G. Jung has given us the notion of the "collective unconscious," Chardin, then, speaks of the "collective conscious."

Chardin waxes poetic (as he often does) when he describes it: "Noosphere...the living membrane which is stretched like a film over the lustrous surface of the star which holds us. An ultimate envelope taking on its own individuality and gradually detaching itself like a luminous aura. This envelope was not only conscious, but thinking...the Very Soul of the Earth."[7] This profound insight reminds us that we are made up of nothing but the material stuff of this planet, that, physically, we *are* this planet. But Chardin goes further: not only are our bodies the stuff of the Earth's body, but our minds are the consciousness of this being, the Earth. We have supposed that we are individuals, yet we "are dust, and to dust ye shall return." We have supposed our minds are our own;

but perhaps, as transpersonal theorists suggest, we are mistaken. Chardin, in fact, argues that it must be so, that "what we are aware of is only the nucleus which is ourselves. The interaction of souls would be incomprehensible if some 'aura' did not extend from one to the other, something proper to each one and common to all." Chardin believes, too, that this consciousness is not only psychological, but of the greatest spiritual importance as well. "Nothing is precious," he says, "Except that part of you which is in other people, and that part of others which is in you. Up there, on high, everything is one."[8]

The Noosphere is a fascinating and intriguing idea, one that many of us desperately want, on some level, to be true. But as we have been describing it thus far, it seems little more than science fiction. How is it that such an awesome phenomenon could possibly come to be? Amazingly, Teilhard predicts the evolution of a machine that hardly even existed in his time beyond being a glorified abacus: the computer. "Here I am thinking," he writes in *Man's Place in Nature*, "of those astonishing electronic machines (the starting-point and hope of the young science of cybernetics), by which our mental capacity to calculate and combine is reinforced and multiplied by a process and to a degree that herald as astonishing advances in this direction as those that optical science has already produced for our power of vision."[9] Teilhard's vision of what computers would do for us is that they would, first, complete our brains, in that in the instantaneous retrieval of information around the globe, what one person lacks is immediately provided by another, and second, they will improve our brains, by facilitating processes more quickly than our own resources can achieve them.[10]

It is also interesting that Chardin predicts the use of the prefix "cyber" in regards to the computer/human matrix, since "cyber" is all the rage in computering circles. In fact, what can be seen as the progenitor of Teilhard's dream of the noosphere is now termed "Cyberspace," in reference to that mystical field of interconnecting computer pathways wherein all of the exchanges are made. As Michael Benedikt describes it in his *Collected Abstracts from the First Conference on Cyberspace*,

Cyberspace is a globally networked, computer-sustained, computer-accessed, and computer-generated, multi-dimensional, artificial, or "virtual" reality. In this world, onto which every computer screen is a window, actual, geographical distance is irrelevant. Objects seen or heard are neither physical nor, necessarily, presentations of physical objects, but are rather—in form, character, and action—made up of data, of pure information. This information is derived in part from the operation of the natural, physical world, but is derived primarily from the immense traffic of symbolic information, images, sounds, and people, that constitute human enterprise in science, art, business, and culture.[11]

The form most of these exchanges take is the computer "bulletin board." On this, any person with the simplest of computers and a modem can call a central, master computer with which literally any number of other users may be linked. Once connected, a person may receive or distribute messages on any given topic to one or a million people. As John Barlow describes it,

In this silent world, all conversation is typed. To enter it, one forsakes both body and place and becomes a thing of words alone. You can see what your neighbors are saying (or recently said), but not what either they or their physical surroundings look like. Town meetings are continuous and discussions range on everything from sexual kinks to depreciation schedules.[12]

And for those who do not traffic on these data expressways, the extent to which they reach is staggering. There are literally thousands of individual bulletin boards around the world, and nearly all of them are linked by one incredible, global bulletin board, the Internet. Sounding like some sinister creation of an Ian Fleming villain, the Internet links more than 8,000 separate bulletin boards and networks, accommodating ten million people around the world.[13] As Jon Katz notes,

Nobody can even calculate how much information is on it, what its boundaries are or who will eventually control it. It contains entire scientific and academic archives, complex networks from aeronautics and African wildlife to the CIA World Factbook. Companies share data between different offices, and hundreds of libraries in dozens of countries are putting their catalogs on it.[14]

Those who study such things predict that the users of the Internet are likely to double each year. Vinton Cerf, designer of the Internet system, says that by the year 2000 there will be more than 100 million users.[15] "This kind of reaching out from any-where in the world," he says, "has got to change the way we think about our world. It will become critical for everyone to be con-nected. Anyone who doesn't will essentially be isolated from the world."[16] And perhaps, in Darwinian terms, be selected out of the emerging node of evolution.

In light of developments such as computer bulletin boards and "super-information highways" like the Internet, Teilhard's fantas-tic notions don't seem so fantastic. He is, it turns out, the unsung prophet of our collective future. It is time that we begin to look forward to what these developments are going to mean to us per-sonally, developmentally. Chardin says that "mankind is now caught up, as though in a train of gears, at the heart of a contin-ually accelerating vortex of self-totalisation." We need to consid-er how the inevitable changes in our natures are going to affect us as individuals, psychologically and pathologically. One advan-tage, though, to facing what is happening to us is that we can stop "groping about" in the dark and take conscious control of our evolution to speed it on its way.

We are, therefore, in the latter twentieth century, at the thresh-old of another great leap in evolution, the contraction and unifi-cation, the construction of the Noosphere, the focusing of our psychic energies. "The powers that we have released," Chardin states in *Human Energy*, "could not possibly be absorbed by the narrow system of individual or national units which the architects of the human Earth have hitherto used. The age of nations has passed. Now unless we wish to perish we must shake off our old prejudices and build the Earth."[17] How we accomplish this is by correcting our errant perception of reality as being made up of separate units. Chardin insists that "to love is to discover and complete one's self in someone other than oneself, an act impos-sible of general realization on Earth so long as each can see in the neighbor no more than a closed fragment following its own course through the world. It is precisely this state of isolation that will end if we begin to discover in each other not merely the elements of one and the same thing, but of a single Spirit in search of Itself."[18]

The result of such a realization is the Noosphere, towards which we are moving even now via our cybernetic interconnections, know it or not, like it or not, want it or not. As our consciousness of unity progresses, the standard of morality will eventually not be placed on the maintenance of private property, but upon the health of the Whole, which will become more and more perceptible to us as Noogenesis unfolds. Chardin himself admits that "these perspectives will appear absurd to those who don't see that life is, from its origins, groping, adventurous, and dangerous. But these perspectives will grow, like an irresistible idea on the horizon of new generations."[19] Indeed, it seems less and less absurd as this very process unfolds before us.

NOTES

1   Gallagher, Blanche. *Meditations with Teilhard de Chardin* (Santa Fe: Bear & Co., 1988), p. 25.

2   Murray, Michael H. *The Thought of Teilhard de Chardin* (New York: Seabury Press, 1966), p. 25.

3   Gallagher, pp. 80-1.

4   *Ibid.*, p. 39.

5   Murray, pp. 20-1.

6   Gallagher, p. 40.

7   *Ibid.*, p. 39.

8   *Ibid.*, p. 105.

9   Chardin, Teilhard de. *Man's Place in Nature* (New York: Harper and Row, 1956), p. 110.

10 *Ibid.*, p. 111.

11 Uncapher, Willard. "Trouble in Cyberspace," *The Humanist* Sept/Oct 1991, p. 9.

12 *Ibid.*, p. 7.

13 Jon Katz. "Bulletin Boards: News from Cyberspace," *Rolling Stone*, April 15, 1993, p. 36.

14 *Ibid.*

15 *Ibid.*

16 *Ibid.*

17 Gallagher, p. 119.

18 *Ibid.*, p. 98.

19 *Ibid.*, p. 135.

PART FOUR

How Religions
Inform Each Other

Strange Bedfellows

Hinduism and Judaic Mysticism in Comparison

I f ever there were strange bedfellows in the field of religion, Hinduism and Judaism are two of the strangest. While there is an abundance of material comparing Christianity and Hinduism, I don't believe I've ever encountered an article or a volume devoted to Hindu-Jewish dialogue. No doubt this is due to their initial seeming dissimilarity. I cannot think of two more divergent systems, yet, as often happens, the closer we look, the more things begin to look familiar.

In both cases we begin with what Michael H. Barnes calls the "archaic" period of religious development. He describes this as a time of "towns with class structure in a larger world, with great and distant gods demanding worship; grand myths; dreams of idealized earthly life; acceptance (and taboo) morality."[1] This describes both cultures well. For both the aboriginal Indian and the Abrahamic Semite, the gods were many and distant. Fate was manipulated by appealing to the gods sacrificially, and the oldest of scriptures in both traditions are those dealing most especially with the protocol of sacrifice.

At this time, Yahweh was one god among many, perhaps, as Bede Griffiths speculates, Yahweh, like Indra, Zeus and Jupiter, was a thunder-god with an appropriate aspect of wrath which has been carried on in the Abrahamic traditions.[2] In any case, it was a long journey for Yahweh in the Israelites' conception from one god among many to the supreme and only god of later Judaism, and nearly as long for Indra to give way to Brahman. For Archaic Hinduism, Indra was the king of the gods, gods which personified elemental forces and could be "bribed" via sacrifices to intervene on behalf of the patron of the sacrifice. It was common, although Indra was admittedly king, to praise many gods in succession as "the highest god." This is called "henotheism," a label archaic Jews shared, although the Hebrew's version of henotheism differed significantly. Their henotheism described Yahweh as one god among many, but understood that Yahweh was the only one with which the Jews were to have any dealings. "Yahweh might not be the only god that existed, his followers said, but he was the only one his people should acknowledge as their god. He could take care of all their needs—war, fertility, and anything else." Michael Barnes continues, saying, "This henotheism was only partially successful. For the next 200 years and more, people were still inclined to hedge their bets, catering to all gods who might have some power."[3]

Eventually, in their respective religions Indra and Yahweh were conceived ultimately as "the king of the Gods," each possessing an intricate tradition of sacrifice and observance, served by an elite class of priests who were the sole mediators between the common person and the divinity. This situation inevitably results in "the creation of a vast abyss, conceived as absolute, between God, the infinite and transcendental Being, and Man, the finite creature. For this reason alone, the rise of institutional religion is more widely removed than any other period from mysticism and all it implies."[4] This estrangement, this separation from the "sky god" away "up there" somewhere (still prevalent in many orthodox Abrahamic traditions) creates a fragmented vision of reality, at which point the culture is ripe for mysticism and the integration it offers. Gershom G. Scholem writes that "mysticism does not deny or overlook the abyss; on the contrary, it begins by realizing its existence, but from there it proceeds to a quest for the secret that will close it in, the hidden path that will span it. It strives to piece together the fragments broken by the religious cataclysm, to bring back the old unity which religion has destroyed.... The soul's path through the abysmal multiplicity of things to the experience of the Divine Reality, now conceived as the primordial unity of all things, becomes its main preoccupation."[5] And so both traditions moved into the "Historic" period of religious development, described by Barnes as being "highly complex civilizations in which people search for the ultimate single Power or Being that encompasses all else; comprehensive and dogmatic theology; hope for a perfect other-worldly existence."[6] While Hinduism's theology moved relatively swiftly into a universalizing mysticism (600 BCE), Judaism took a thousand-year detour before reaching this goal.

Which is not to say that there was no progress for the Jewish believer, just that it took much time for the mystical ideas common to both traditions to develop for the Jews. The Jewish henotheism was finally broken by the exile into Babylon (300 BCE) where the Jews finally relinquished the notion that gods were territorial. Yahweh went into exile with them; thus, it was slavery which convinced the Jews of Yahweh's supremacy. (So prevalent was the notion of divine terratorialism that when a foreigner converted to serving Yahweh, he returned to his own land with two carts-full of soil from Israel so that Yahweh would not leave him).[7] For the next thousand years, between the Maccobean revolt, the Roman destruction of Jerusalem, and the diaspora, the Jews had a tough enough time maintaining their cultural integrity to go much beyond their post-exilic synagogal tradition. What mysticism there was took the form of apocalyptic visions in which the heathens and the gentiles "get what's coming to them." When, in medieval rabbinicalism, mysticism as an interior process began to develop in earnest, it started out in the same way it did for the Hindus—as a "secret doctrine."

The *Svetasvatara Upanishad* informs us of "that which is hidden in the secret of the Vedas, even the Mystic Doctrines...."[8] The new mysticism claimed as its source the old sacrificial scriptures. Scholem says, "Instead of the one act of Revelation, there is a constant repetition of this act. This new Revelation...the mystic tries to link up with the sacred texts of the old; hence the new interpretation given to the canonical texts and sacred books of the great religions."[9] For the Jew, the primary text of Jewish mysticism, the *Zohar*, informs us that "the *Torah* has two sides: that which is disclosed and that which is undisclosed, that which is hidden and that which is revealed."[10] In such a way, new meanings were read into many of the old scriptures (not just the Torah, exclusively), and in them the Jewish mystic found a manual aiding him in sensory detachment (*Ecclesiastes*), the heights and depths of spiritual struggle (*Psalms*), and the union of the individual soul with the Universal Soul (*Song of Songs*).[11]

In both traditions, the mystical doctrines were held as secrets that could only be approached by the learned few (a Jewish man cannot study Kabbalah—Jewish mysticism—until he is thirty). The initiate soon learns that this dual nature of the scriptures has further-reaching implications. The Hindu discovers the doctrine of Parusha and Prakriti. According to the *Svetasvatara Upanishad*, Brahman is known in three aspects: the Lord (*parusha*), the self, and Nature (*prakriti*).[12] *Parusha* is the transcendent aspect of the divine, and *Prakriti* the embodied manifestation. The *Brihad-Aranyaka Upanishad* describes it thus: "There are, assuredly, two forms of Brahma: the formed and the formless, the mortal and the immortal, the stationary and the moving, the actual and the yon."[13] The *Zohar* echoes this in saying "The process of creation, too, has taken place on two planes...the lower corresponds to the higher; one produced the upper world (of the Sephiroth), the other the nether world (of the visible creation).[14] "The *Zohar* expressly distinguished between two worlds, which both represent God—first a primary world, the most deeply hidden of all, which remains insensible and unintelligible to all but God...and secondly one, joined unto the first, which makes it possible to know God, and of which the Bible says: 'Open ye the gates that I may enter,' the world of attributes."[15]

God having attributes is a sticky subject for some in both traditions. The *Zohar* explicitly states, "Woe to the man who should make bold to identify the Lord with any single attribute.[16] ...Neither shape nor form has he and no vessel exists to contain him, nor any means to apprehend him."[17] Yet the *Zohar* also says, "If one contemplates the things in mystical meditation, everything is revealed as one,"[18] and describes God as "the Soul of the soul." The *Chandogya Upanishad* says that Brahman is "containing all works, containing all desires, containing all odors, containing all tastes, encompassing this whole world, the unspeaking, the unconcerned—this is the Soul of mine within the heart, this is Brahma,"[19] and describes God as "the Real of the real."[20] The Hassidic "Song of Unity" sings, "Everything is in Thee, and Thou art in everything; Thou fillest everything and dost encompass it."[21] And again, from the *Upanishads*, "Brahma before, Brahma behind, to right and to left. Stretched forth below and above, Brahma, indeed, is this whole world, this widest extent."[22] This rides the border between dualism and monism, and both traditions have many proponents on either side. We will not document these tensions, but will acknowledge that they have created great struggles indeed within their traditions.

Also common in their conception of the relationship of the divine to the temporal is the doctrine of emanation. The "sephiroth" mentioned in the paragraph above is one of ten "emanations" of the divine, each embodying some attribute of Yahweh, and which pervade and contain the material and spiritual worlds. The *Upanishads* in two places paint for us a vivid image of this emanation in the spider, who "might come out with his thread as small sparks come forth from the fire, even so from this Soul come forth all vital energies, all worlds, all gods, all beings."[23]

The source of being in both mystical traditions is also the same: nothing. The *Rig Veda* says, "There was then neither being nor non-being....without breath breathed by its own power, That One."[24] "It is this mystical 'nothingness,'" says Scholem, "from which all the other stages of God's gradual unfolding in the Sephiroth emanate and which the Kabbalists call the highest Sephira, or the 'supreme crown' of Divinity."[25] (It is interesting to note, as Scholem does, that the Hebrew word for "nothing," *ain*, has the same consonants as the word for "I", *ani*.[26])

The Kabbalist conceived eventually of an indifferent Divinity, which they called "the Root of all Roots," the "Great Reality" or

"Indifferent Unity." But most especially, Scholem says, this was called En-Sof. "The latter designation reveals the impersonal character of this aspect of the hidden God from the standpoint of man.... It signifies 'the infinite' as such; not; as has been frequently suggested, 'He who is infinite' but 'That which is infinite.' Kabbalism abandons the personalistic basis of the Biblical conception of God."[27] Thus, in both traditions, the conception of God as celestial monarch gave way to the perception of divine immanence of all worlds.

Both traditions play with microcosm/macrocosm and seek to identify humanity in various ways with the Divine. "In the beginning," says the *Brihad-Aranyaka Upanishad*, "this world was Soul alone in the form of a Person. Looking around, he saw nothing else than himself. He said first 'I am.' Thence arose the name 'I.'"[28] For the Kabbalists, "the world of God the Creator is capable of being visualized under the image of man the created. From this it follows that the limbs of the human body...are nothing but images of a certain spiritual mode of existence which manifests itself in the symbolic figure of Adam Kadmon, the primordial man."[29] Scholem continues, saying "God in the most deeply hidden of His manifestations...is called 'He.' God in the complete unfolding of his Being, Grace and Love, in which He becomes capable of being perceived by the 'reason of the heart'...is called 'You.' But God in His supreme manifestation, where the fullness of His Being finds its final expression in the last and all-embracing of His attributes, is called 'I.'"[30] The Universal Soul manifested as the Divine Man, the great "I Am" of both traditions, is an important development in that humans reciprocate the making of humanity after God's own image. We recognize God in our image, too, and the primal abyss or estrangement is experienced as breached. "The Man has a thousand heads," say the *Vedas*, "a thousand eyes, a thousand feet. He pervaded the earth on all sides and extended beyond it...It is the Man who is all this, whatever has been and whatever is to be. He is the ruler of immortality."[31] The *Svetasvatara Upanishad* elaborates, "I know this mighty Person (Parusha) ...Only by knowing Him does one pass over death. There is no other path for going there."[32]

The previous verse referred to "knowing" as having salvific value. Indeed, cognition is a means of salvation in both traditions. For the Jewish mystic, "the rational faculty latent in the mind is actualized in the process of cognition, and this realization of the intellect is the sole guide to immortality...by acquiring it, the Kabbalist thus realizes something of the divine in his own nature.... It is only by penetrating into the mysteries of the Torah, that is to say, through the mystical realization of his cognitive powers, that he acquires it."[33] For the Hindu, "the discipline of knowing," or *jnana yoga,* is one of the primary paths to salvation. According to the *Svetasvatara Upanishad,* "By knowing what is therein, Brahma-knowers become merged in Brahma, intent theron, liberated from the womb [rebirth]."[34]

As far as the conception of exactly what it is that is saved, we also find some parallels. According to the *Zohar,* there are three distinct spiritual agencies: "*Nefesh*—which is life—is the lowest of the three."[35] This is similar to "life" in the *Upanishads, prana,* or "breath." "The gods do breathe along with breath," says the *Taittiriya Upanishad,* "As also men and beasts. For truly, breath is the life of beings, therefore it is called the Life-of-all."[36]

The second agent is called by the *Zohar* "*Ruah*—which is spirit—[and] is a grade higher."[37] Now *Ruah* is the Hebrew word for "breath." The parallels are not perfect analogs, but the same work is obviously going on here. The *Zohar's* use of *ruah* is probably most similar to *hamsa* in the *Upanishads,* perhaps the elemental soul of the *Maitri Upanishad* (3.2).

Ultimately, we come to "*Neshamah*—which is the holy soul...[that] dominates the others," as the *Zohar* reads.[38] For the Hindu this is the Supreme Brahman/Atman at the heart of all things.

It is the presence of the Atman in all things that connects us. It is by agency of the Atman that it can be said that Brahma is all. This is not a clear conception in the Upanishads. Different writers seem to have divergent opinions, but it is this view which makes the most sense (at least to this writer). Ground-breaking Kabbalist (speculated to be the author of the *Zohar*) Moses de Leon has written, "Everything is linked with everything else down to the lowest ring on the chain, and the true essence of God is above as well as below, in the heavens and on the earth, and nothing exists outside Him.... When God opened the *Torah* to Israel, He opened the seven heavens to them, and they saw that nothing was there in reality but His Glory.... God's essence is linked and connected with all worlds...all forms of existence are linked and connected with each other, but derived from His existence and essence."[39]

Eventually this sense of connectedness combined with the prior concept of the duality of God's nature to produce a doctrine for the Kabbalists surprisingly like the left hand path of Tantra. The *Zohar* says, "And they flowed in a straight path through all the spheres, until they came to that one place which collects them all into a union of male and female, and that one place is called the foundation, for it is the life and breath of all worlds."[40] For the Jew, the image of Shiva and Shakti were represented by Yaweh (the masculine, transcendent element of God) and his holy bride, the Shekinah (the feminine, immanent element of God). Of this union in Hinduism, Thomas Hopkins says, "Shakti is present in all things, in the forbidden food and drink and especially in sexual intercourse. Shakti is the Goddess, the eternal female partner. The danger is that men fail to recognize their human partner as the Goddess, and use her to gratify their senses. They should instead worship her, or the Goddess in her, and turn their senses from gratification of selfish desires to an expression of devotion. This...can be done by means of a disciplined ritual."[41] The Kabbalists are not quite as formal, for in their estimation, "every true marriage is a symbolical realization of the union of God and the Shekhinah.... The Kabbalists deduced from Genisis 4:1, 'And Adam knew Eve his wife' that 'knowledge' always means the realization of a union, be it that of wisdom (or reason) and intelligence, or that of the King and the Shekhinah. Thus knowledge itself received a sublime erotic quality...and this point is often stressed in Kabbalistic writings."[42]

Another similarity of these Historic religions is the numinous quality accorded to the scriptures of the prior period. The Archaic scriptures of the Jews (the *Torah*) and of the Hindus (the *Vedas*) both assume nearly divine status after each tradition underwent their mystical evolutions. Hopkins said of the Hindus that "Knowledge of the natural world has become secondary to the knowledge of holy speech." The *Chandogya Upanishad* contains a hymn to the Vedas which describes them as the sweetest of celestial honey. Worlds are created, destroyed, and maintained through the power of words. The *Zohar* tells a similar tale: "The *Torah* it was that created the angels and created all the worlds and through *Torah* all are sustained. The world could not endure the *Torah*."[43] Elsewhere, it reads, "Whoever studies *Torah* each day has a share in the world to come, and is himself considered a builder of worlds, for through *Torah* the world was built and completed. Thus, whoever studies *Torah*, not only completes the world, but sustains it."[44] So, in both traditions, we see the emergence of an occult science of language. Soon, the words themselves were being employed in order to manipulate various forces of manifest and spiritual realities. The *Taittiriya Upanishad* says, "These are the great combinations. He who knows these combinations, thus expounded, becomes conjoined with offspring, with cattle, with pre-eminence in sacred knowledge, with food, with the heavenly world."[45] Powerful indeed! "Hebrew, according to the Kabbalists, reflects the fundamental spiritual nature of the world...it has a mystical value.... All creation...is...nothing but an expression of His hidden self that begins and ends by giving itself a name, the holy name of God, the perpetual act of creation."[46] Scholem elsewhere says "*Torah*...is the cosmic law of the Universe.... Each configuration of letters in it, whether it makes sense in human speech or not, symbolizes some aspect of God's creative power which is active in the universe."[47] So serious were they that one ancient Kabbalist, the prophetic Abufalia, said, "One has to be most careful not to move a consonant or vowel from its position, for if he errs in reading the letter commanding a certain member, that member may be torn away and may change its place or alter its nature immediately and be transformed into a different shape so that in consequence that person may become a cripple."[48]

Perhaps the most startling revelation of this study to someone thinking they are familiar with the Abrahamic faiths is the discovery of the Jewish Kabbalistic doctrine of reincarnation. "He...who has not understanding," says the *Kata Upanishad,* "who is unmindful and ever impure, reaches not the goal, but goes on to reincarnation. He, however, who has understanding, who is mindful and ever pure, reaches the goal from which he is born no more."[49] This is standard Hindu stuff, but what are we to make of the inexplicable appearance of such a doctrine in Judaism? The Jewish theory of Gilgul (revolving) appears first in the twelfth century *Book Bahir.* According to Charles Ponce, "all souls must undergo transmigration and that the souls of men revolve like a stone which is thrown from a sling, so many turns before the final release.... Because all souls were originally contained in Adam, or actually made up the soul of Adam, the objective of each individual soul was to win its place back in the soul of Adam, and by so doing restore him to his original form before the Fall."[50]

For both traditions, great import is placed upon scholarliness (especially for the rabbinic and priestly folk), the attendance to the written word, and chanting. The spiritual process itself has some similarities. The goal of the Hassidic Jew, according to the eighteenth century Hassidic philosopher, Maggid of Mezerich, is this: "A man should actually detach his ego from his body until he has passed through all the worlds and become one with God, till he disappears entirely out of the bodiless world." The *Prasna Upanishad* describes this more poetically, saying "As these flowing rivers that tend toward the ocean, on reaching the ocean, disappear, their name and form are destroyed, and it is called simply 'the ocean.'"[51] Techniques for accomplishing this are likewise similar. To quote Scholem again, "[Abulifa's] teachings represent but a Judaized version of the...Indian...system known as Yoga. To cite only one instance out of many, an important part in Abulafia's system is played by the technique of breathing.... Abulifia lays down certain rules of body posture, certain corresponding combinations of consonants and vowels, and certain forms of recitation."[52]

Jewish mystics have not been slack in taking their mysticism forward, either, for they have continued beyond the orthodox system of Hinduism to mirror developments of the Jains (Ari Luria carefully avoided harming even insects and worms, insisting that these too would evolve through the course of transmigrating souls), and the Buddhists (Luria taught that "once the purified, humbled mind had attached itself to its divine source, it was obliged to plunge downward into the descending worlds with renewed strength and withdraw the holy sparks from the husks of matter encasing every being, flower, mineral, and demon inhabiting them."[53] What a mental image—black-clad Jewish Bhodisattvas flying like Superman between the worlds!).

What began as a whim became something of an obsession: the idea that mysticism in any cultural context is going to eventually develop in nearly identical patterns is frightening to the Abrahamic orthodox. It is, though, another proof of Huxley's Perennial Philosophy, and of our unity as People of Faith, regardless of our religion of origin. These historic developments are the accepted norms in their respective traditions, Hinduism and Judaism (although most Christians would be loathe to believe it of their mother faith). Perhaps Jewish/Hindu dialogue is not such a silly proposition, but an avenue of important investigation as we try to close the gaps between the East and West.

> "And thus the substance of the canonical texts,
> like that of all other religious values,
> is melted down and given another form as
> it passes through the fiery stream of the
> mystical consciousness. It is hardly surprising
> that, hard as the mystic may try to remain
> within the confines of his religion, he often
> consciously or unconsciously approaches,
> or even transgresses, its limits."[54]
>
> —Gershom G. Scholem

NOTES

1   Barnes, Michael H. *In the Presence of Mystery* (Mystic: XXIII Publications, 1984), p. 6.

2   Griffiths, Bede. *The Marriage of East and West* (Springfield: Templgate Publishers, 1982), p. 106.

3   Barnes, p. 50.

4   Scholem, Gershom G. *Major Trends in Jewish Mysticism* (New York: Schocken Books, 1946), p. 7.

5   *Ibid.*

6   Barnes, p. 6.

7   *II Kings,* chap. 5.

8   Hume, Robert Ernest, trans. *The Thirteen Principal Upanishads* (Delhi: Oxford University Press, 1877), p. 406.

9   Scholem, p. 9.

10 Winston, Jerry, trans. *Colors from the Zohar* (San Francisco: Barah, 1976), p. 57.

11 Epstein, Perle. *Kabbalah: The Way of the Jewish Mystic* (Boston: Shambhala, 1978), 11.

12 Hopkins, Thomas J. *The Hindu Religious Tradition* (Belmont: Wadsworth Publishing Co., 1971), p. 66.

13 Hume, *Brihad-Aranyaka Upanishad* 2.3.1, p. 97.

14 *Zohar* I.240b, quoted by Scholem, p. 222.

15 Scholem, p. 208.

16 Scholem, Gershom G., ed., *Zohar: The Book of Splendor* (New York: Schocken, 1963), p. 78.

17 *Ibid*, p. 79.

18 *Zohar* 1.24a, quoted by Scholem, p. 222.

19 Hume, *Chandogya Upanishad* 3.14.4, p. 210.

20 *Ibid., Brihad-Aranyaka Upanishad* 2.1.20, p. 95.

21 Scholem, p. 108.

22 Hume, *Mundaka Upanishad* 2.2.11, p. 373.

23 *Ibid., Brihad-Aranyaka Upanishad* 2.1.20, p. 95.

24 *Ibid., Rig Veda* 10.129.1-2, p. 13.

25 Scholem, p. 217.

26 *Ibid.*, p. 218.

27 *Ibid.*, p. 141.

28 Hume, *Brihad-Aranyaka Upanishad* 1.4.1, p. 81.

29 Scholem, p. 215.

30 *Ibid.*, p. 216.

31 O'Flaherty, Wendy Doniger, trans. *The Rig Veda* (New York: Penguin, 1982), 10.90.1-7, p. 29.

32 Hume, *Svetasvatara Upanishad* 3.10, p. 401.

33 Scholem, p. 240-1.

34 Hume, *Svetasvatara Upanishad* 1.7, p. 395.

35 Winston, p. 43.

36 Hume, *Taittiriya Upanishad* 3.1, p. 284.

37 Winston, p. 43.

38 *Ibid.*

39 Scholem, p. 223.

40 Winston, p. 34.

41 Hopkins, p. 129.

42 Scholem, p. 235.

43 *Zohar*, p. 121.

44 Winston, p. 68.

45 Hume, *Taittiriya Upanishad* 1.3.4, p. 276.

46 Scholem, p. 43.

47 *Ibid.*, p. 14.

48 *Ibid.*, p. 138.

49 Hume, *Katha Upanishad* 3.7-8, p. 352.

50 Ponce, Charles. *Kabbalah* (Wheaton: Theosophical Publishing House, 1973), p.215.

51 Hume, *Prasna Upanishad* 6.5, p. 389.

52 Scholem, p. 139.

53 Epstein, p. 20.

54 Scholem, p. 9.

Bede Griffiths

Holy Man for Our Time

"The holy man of our time, it seems, is not a figure like Gotama Buddha or Jesus or Mohammed, a man who could found a world religion, but a figure like Gandhi, a man who passes over by sympathetic understanding from his own religion to other religions and comes back again with new insight to his own. Passing over and coming back, it seems, is the spiritual adventure of our time."

More than any other single person I know of, Bede Griffiths exemplifies the above statement by John S. Dunne. He is a quiet man, yet with a powerful undercurrent that charges the air with electricity in his presence. He is unusually tall, and frighteningly thin. He wears the saffron robe of a Hindu sannyasi (holy man), and is respected as such by Hindus and Christians alike.

Bede's story really begins with two priests from France, Jules Monchanin and Henri Le Saux, who had a dream of founding the monastic life in India in 1947. They soon found that what monks in the West considered poverty was relatively luxurious in comparison with normal Indian life. Monks are used to being limited to a bed, table, chair, and bookshelf. Possession of such luxuries separated them from the people, and so even the most basic furniture was prohibited. The two monks ate only vegetarian food, which they begged for, and were forbidden alcohol—another Hindu prohibition. They ate on the floor on plates of leaves, and could be distinguished from Hindu sannyassis only by the rosaries they wore around their necks.

Jules Monchanin eventually took the name Swami Parama Arubi Anandam (the Bliss of the Supreme Spirit) and Henri Le Saux was called Swami Abhishiktananda (the Bliss of Christ). They also tried valiantly to bridge the gap separating the two traditions. The two monks met with dubious success. There were a number of false starts and outright failures for their efforts. In fact, at the time of their deaths, they had little to show for their many years of hard labor. Their work would not reach fruition until they had passed their mantle to a monk named Bede in the 1960s.

Bede was born in 1906 to a young English and properly Anglican couple. His life was pretty uneventful until he went to Oxford and began to study under one of the twentieth century's greatest Christian theologians, C.S. Lewis. Neither of them was Christian at the time, but both of them were driven in that direction through transcendental aspects of English literature. Bede had constructed a whole religion based on Wordsworth as prophet. Even after he left school, he and Lewis, both undergoing profound spiritual transformations, corresponded regularly.

Bede found that he wanted to get as close to the primal as possible, to live in the pristine state of nature that his poetry conjured for him. So, with a couple of friends, he moved into a cottage in the Cotswolds. They lived spare lives there. No cars, radios, phonographs, or any other convenience devices. They walked where they wanted to go and read poetry aloud as their sole entertainment and inspiration. Then Bede made a mistake: he decided to read the Psalms as poetry. He never recovered, and finding that he loved monastic life—since it was essentially what he was already doing—he eventually decided to become a Christian monk. He tried to be Anglican, for his mother's sake, but it didn't sit well with him, and despite great familial turbulence, became what many Protestant mothers fear worst of all: a Roman Catholic.

He joined Prinknash Abbey near Gloucester. He took to the mode of life quickly, and loved it. It was here that he began to study Eastern philosophy, and fell in love with it. So when an opportunity came about to help secure the monastic life in India, he responded eagerly. It wouldn't do to go into the long list of various ashrams and their permutations that he and the other monks went through. Suffice to say, in the late seventies, something incredible had taken shape in the community known as Shantivanam. It was Bede's hope to have created a center where people of different religious traditions could meet together in an atmosphere of prayer and learn to grow together towards that unity in Truth which is the goal of all religion. A visitor described it thus:

> The sun rising over the River Cauvery would find individuals and small groups meditating on its banks. Breakfast was preceded by community worship in the temple. The vegetarian meals were eaten Indian style, without utensils, on the floor of an unfurnished dining hall, and though ample they were simple to the point of austerity. Five times a day the community gathered in the temple to meditate and chant Hindu, Buddhist, and Christian prayers. The Mass of the Indian Rite which was used in the ashram reflected the cosmic symbolism of Hinduism. At the offertory, water was sprinkled around the gifts and the altar, then upon the people. The celebrant himself took a sip to purify himself within. In the bread and wine, the fruits of the Earth and the work of human hands were offered to the Divine. Next, eight flowers were placed around the gifts in the eight directions of space to signify that the sacrifice offered was at the center of the universe. Then incense was waved over the gifts as was fire, the flame of burning camphor. The fourfold offering of the elements was used to signify that the Mass was a cosmic sacrifice. Christ had assumed the whole Creation and was offering it in and through himself to the Creator. It was also a reflection of the fact that in India everything is acknowledged to have a sacred character.
>
> In the temple here, as in Hindu temples throughout India, worshippers could mark their foreheads with colored powders steeped in

symbolism. In the morning, a paste of sandalwood, a very precious wood which spreads its fragrance to others even when cut with an axe, was used to signify the grace of God; at midday, a red powder, kumkum, was used to mark a third eye upon the forehead, the eye of internal knowledge and intuitive experience of God; in the evening, vibhudi, ashes, served as a reminder of human mortality and of the purified self, for in ashes all impurities had been burnt away. The design and symbolism of the building itself belonged to another world of symbols, strange and bewildering at first to the western visitor.

—Kathryn Spink, *A Sense of the Sacred*

Fr. Bede believes that it is no longer possible for religious traditions to exist in isolation. They must now enter into dialogue with each other. "It is no longer a question of a Christian going about to convert others to the faith," he says, "but of each one being ready to listen to the other and so to grow together in mutual understanding.... God has graced every tradition with insight into the divine mystery, from the most primitive to the most sophisticated—each has a gift to bring to the world." Bede says that his goal has been to "set the orthodox tradition of the Christian faith alongside the orthodox tradition of Vedanta and to see how they can mutually enrich one another."

Bede has published many series of lectures on the *Upanishads* and Vedanta, and has written a commentary on the *Bhagavhad Gita*. Most rewarding as far as understanding his own position, though, is his own commentary on the various Vedantic commentators, Sankara, Ramanuja, and Madhva (Bede's book *Vedanta and Christian Faith,* Dawn Horse Press, 1973, is highly recommended).

In a way, one could say that Bede has attempted an impossible task: to build a bridge between two of the most diverse traditions the world has ever known. His work has been twofold: to represent Christianity to non-Christian faith communities without the typical sneer of superiority, and to represent Hinduism to Christians in a way that is neither threatening nor heterodox. For these awesome accomplishments he deserves great thanks and recognition for the true missionary he has been. He has also broken much ground upon which we must build as we begin a third millennium, learning to share our wisdom with our sister faith traditions, and perhaps more importantly, learning to receive theirs.

The Way
of Non-Direction

Insights on Spiritual Direction from the Tao Te Ching

Often in my ministry, I find words from the Hindu *Upanishads* or the Taoist *Tao Te Ching* popping into my head, sometimes at exactly the right moment. In ruminating on some of these "little revelations" I have started thinking about what insights other traditions not normally associated with Christian spiritual direction might have to offer to its practice. I have decided to limit my comments to one tradition from which I have drawn much spiritual nurture and counsel: Taoism.

Taoism (pronounced "Dow-ism") is a native religion of China, and has as its principal scripture the *Tao Te Ching,* a book of Chinese philosophical poetry containing eighty-one pieces, written sometime between the seventh and the fourth centuries B.C.E. According to tradition, it was written by a quiet librarian named Lao Tzu.

The person who practices Taoism sees herself as equal to all other created things, and in fact, gleans all wisdom from observing nature. Nature is correct. Humans think too much and that gets us into trouble. Nature reveals the essence of the Tao. The Tao is a part of nature, or more accurately, nature is a part of the Tao; and therefore, the Tao is not personified, like the Christian God. It is impersonal, like a principle or a force. This might

141

sound negative, even irreconcilable to a Judeo-Christian concept of God, but it is neither negative nor irreconcilable. In fact, the Tao is God as nature sees God. The sparrow, for instance, does not have a "personal relationship" with God. She does not perceive God as a personality, but as the very web of being in which she moves and of which she consists: the wind beneath her wings, the worm in the ground, the dry sheltered branch in the storm. Similarly, the Taoist follows this example and perceives God not as a personal deity, but through the web of his or her experience of the world and through the nature of things.

By observing nature, the Taoist understands the Way of the Tao and seeks to walk in that same way. A person who is generally regarded as being good at this is often referred to as a "sage," whose function was often to guide people into spiritual truth, similar in some ways to the ministry of the spiritual director. Like a carpenter who knows that it is easier to saw with the grain of the wood than against it, the sage knows that when one lives in cooperation with nature and the Tao, one's life can be free from stressful striving, and one can find contentment by resting in the "Way" things are.

"Sin" in Taoism is going against the grain, and one's punishment is immediate and in this world: a life of stress and struggle. "Salvation" is going with the flow, finding a life of freedom and security, because one knows how the universe works and can cooperate with it. There is no "guilt" language in the *Tao Te Ching*. The Tao's love is universal and unconditional. It is not for the enlightened only, or the holy, or even the moral. The Tao is there for all. "It is the good person's treasure," Lao Tzu writes, "and the bad person's refuge... Why did the sages of old value the Tao so much? Because when you seek, you find. And when you sin, you are forgiven."

Taoism and the Spiritual Life: Being and Non-Being

The *Tao Te Ching* speaks of matter and spirit as if they were partners, one incapable of functioning without the other. Taoists speak of spirit as "non-being," implying something that exists in objective reality, but which possesses no physical manifestation, or "being." Synonyms for spirit/"non-being" are emptiness and non-existence. Meister Eckhart in the Christian tradition spoke in similar terms when he said that "God is a being beyond being and a nothingness beyond being."[1] This unitive vision of spirituality is difficult for Westerners reared with pervasive dualism. Lao Tzu asks, as if speaking directly to us, "Being both body and spirit, can you embrace unity and not be fragmented?" (Poem 10).

To illustrate his vision, Lao Tzu presents non-being as absolutely necessary for physical realities to "function," and vice versa, saying, "Thirty spokes join together at one hub, but it is the hole in the center that makes it operable. Clay is molded into a pot, but it is the emptiness inside that makes it useful. Doors and windows are cut to make a room, but it is the empty spaces that we use" (Poem 11).

The first time I read these verses, chills ran down my spine. I felt that I had been told a great secret that was the most obvious thing in the world: the relationship between matter and spirit. One is not dominant. "Existence and non-existence produce one another," Lao Tzu explains, "Existence is what we have, but non-existence is what we use."

In addition to non-being, which is thing, or noun-oriented, Lao Tzu also offers a matching concept which is action, or verb-oriented: non-action. The Chinese word for non-action is *wu-wei*. *Wu-wei* literally means "not doing," but it has many applications.

With this concept, Lao Tzu speaks directly to twentieth century Westerners and our fast-paced culture. He tells us, "If you spend your life filling your senses and rushing around 'doing' things, you will be beyond hope." It is difficult for some of us to slow down and not feel guilty.

Instead, Lao Tzu asks a difficult question: "When Heaven gives and takes away, can you be content to just let things come or go? And even when you understand all things, can you simply allow yourself to be?" (Poem 10).

Lao Tzu promises, "Who can wait for the storm to stop, to find peace in the calm that follows? The person who is able to wait patiently in this peace will eventually know what is right" (Poem 15).

Slowing down enough to hear the voice of the Spirit, or to observe the Way of the Tao, is in my experience one of the most important spiritual disciplines of all. An old joke reminds us that Westerners say, "Don't just sit there, do something!" while Eastern wisdom says, "Don't just do something, sit there!"

The value of not-doing is every bit as great as the value of non-being, or spirit, and the health of our non-being/spirit is utterly dependent upon our ability to not-do.

Taoism and Spiritual Direction: The Power of Water

The Tao Te Ching concerns itself greatly with leadership, both political and spiritual. Not surprisingly, Lao Tzu astounds us with a parable about the power of water:

> In the whole World nothing is softer than water. Even those who succeed when attacking the hard and the strong cannot overcome it, because nothing can harm it. The weak overcomes the strong, the soft conquers the hard. No one in the World can deny this, yet no one seems to know how to put it into practice (Poem 78).

The ability to be strong in the way that water is strong is a mystery that Lao Tzu says no one can quite grasp, and yet it is nonetheless the only way to be truly successful. Even though no one "knows how" to do it, truly spiritual people seem to evidence this power without trying: "The sagely person is like water," Lao Tzu says. "Water benefits all things and does not compete with them. It gathers in unpopular places. In this it is like the Tao" (Poem 8).

Learning to be like water involves the practice of *wu-wei*. Unlike just learning "not-doing" as we discussed above, *wu-wei* calls us to a deeper understanding that might be called "not-forcing."

The Taoist watches nature and sees that what nature does— building mountains, growing forests, making rivers, birthing cubs—is accomplished effortlessly. Being one with the Tao, nature goes its own way and forces nothing; and yet grand works and great beauty result. *Wu-wei*, therefore, isn't inactive at all, but is activity at its most efficient, because it accomplishes without effort. When the sage, recognizing oneness with the Tao, acts upon his or her environment in the spirit of the Tao, then, as Thomas Merton writes,

> His [or her] action is not a violent manipulation of exterior reality, an "attack" on the outside world, bending it to his conquering will: on the contrary, he respects external reality by yielding to it...a perfect accomplishment of what is demanded by the precise situation.

When it comes to the issue of leadership, especially spiritual leadership and spiritual direction, Lao Tzu asks us pointedly, "Loving all people and leading them well, can you do this without imposing your will?" This is a great and important question for us, who are surrounded by traditions notorious for spiritual coercion. Unfortunately, we often unwittingly perpetuate the cycle of coercion. It is easy for us to think that the answers we have found after our own many years of search and struggle are the "right" answers for everybody. But Taoism suggests that, like water, all things simply flow out and return, void of any notions of "right" or "wrong."

The key to being successful in spiritual leadership, according to Lao Tzu, is to not try. "Therefore the sage, not trying, cannot fail," says Lao Tzu. "Not clutching, she cannot lose." Likewise in our own spiritual lives, "the truly good person does not try to be good." Goodness needs to come naturally, effortlessly, like breathing or hearing. The sage is not concerned with being good, or even with being a good spiritual director. He or she does not give it a thought. It is not a goal. The goal is to respond humanely— as a human would—to whatever situation life gives.

This advice is congruent with the attitudes of other spiritual directors I know, but I have rarely heard these principles expressed so clearly or evocatively. Most spiritual directors would not dream of "forcing" their directees into a practice before they are ready, nor would most initiate violent interventions into the lives of their directees. But it is sometimes difficult to articulate why we believe this.

A gift of the *Tao Te Ching* is not only giving us words to describe our experiences, but illuminating what we already know. Lao Tzu might be speaking specifically about a spiritual director when he writes, "The sage who leads says: 'I practice "not-doing" and the people transform themselves. I enjoy peace and the people correct themselves. I stay out of their business affairs and the people prosper. I have no desires and the people, all by themselves, become simple and honest.'"

Non-Attachment

Lao Tzu also advocates good spiritual direction technique by suggesting that we let directees make their own discoveries. Instead of telling them what they need to know, it is far more effective for directees themselves to make the associations and experience the epiphanies. As Lao Tzu says, "The best leader puts great value in words and says little, so that when his work is finished the people all say, 'We did it ourselves!'"

It is best for us not to put too much stock in developmental theories or personality systems, since in pursuing the effectiveness they offer, they can sometimes blind us to what is going on for directees in the here and now. Lao Tzu warns: "When you organize, you must of necessity use names and order. But given that, you must also know where to leave off naming and structuring. Knowing when to stop, you can avoid danger" (Poem 32).

It is difficult for us to simply let go of the end result, to not strive or push a directee, especially if we are impatient with his or her "progress." We may have somehow come to believe that conversion is an instantaneous occurrence. In reality, however, this is almost never the case. Conversion is a slow, difficult process; the seeds that were planted years ago slowly take root, and even more slowly blossom. Much of the time we may not even be aware of just when conversion is occurring because, in a sense, it is happening underground, like the developing seed. As directors, we need to trust that the Spirit constantly whispers to all people, and needs little help from us. We would do well to relinquish our attachment to the outcome of a single session or even the duration of a directee's involvement with us. This is difficult because as we sit with people, hear their struggles, and get to know their foibles, we begin to love them. We care so much for the people we minister to that we are often unaware of the ways we attach ourselves to their "progress" and growth.

Lao Tzu counsels that we should give of ourselves to others without any hope of success or fear of failure: "The sage makes good on his half of the deal and demands nothing of others." The sage is not concerned with getting anything back because with the Tao all things flow out and return. This is not to say that we should not care about people; rather we should not be attached to immediate results. To care, to love, to invest ourselves in others is part of what makes us human and holy. Lao Tzu says, "The sage's heart is not set in stone. She is as sensitive to the people's feelings as to her own. She says, 'To people who are good, I am good. And to people who are not good? I am good to them, too.' This is true goodness. 'People who are trustworthy, I trust. And people who are not trustworthy, I also trust.' This is real trust" (Poem 49). If we can learn this kind of trust in the nature of things, I believe we can be more effective listeners and companions.

Humility

Perhaps the most important truth Lao Tzu has to teach spiritual leaders is humility. Potential directees come to us because we are "people in the know," who they often believe are "spiritually advanced" and able to help them begin the journey.

The truth, which most if not all spiritual directors know well, is that we are all beginners; much of what we have come to know simply reveals how little we actually do know. Lao Tzu tells us, "Those who know, do not speak. Those who speak, do not know" (Poem 56). Those concerned about directing with integrity and holiness find that spiritual maturity simply increases our awareness of our shared humanity and leads to a more compassionate rapport with the directee. As the Christian mystic Mechtilde of Magdeburg says, we should live "welcoming to all," expecting to learn as much from our directees as we hope they may learn from us.[2]

The goal for any spiritual director is to maintain a genuine and vital relationship with God and the universe, and then to attend to others' spiritual lives. Lao Tzu tells us that "One who is well grounded will not be uprooted. One who has a firm embrace will not let go."

Both grounding and embracing are essential. Grounded in our tradition, we will not be led astray; embracing the traditions of others, we inherit vast wisdom. My spiritual experience as a Christian need not be divorced from my study of Taoism. Cultivating relationships with the wisdom of other traditions informs and enriches our practice in so many ways: by adding to our repertoire of God-images, by enlarging our understanding of how others experience the divine presence, and by augmenting our world-view with other models and potentialities. Nothing external impacts us as greatly as taking in the wisdom of others - be it a directee's observations or the great Lao Tzu's - and allowing those seeds to germinate deep in the soil of our own spiritual garden.

Non-being, non-action, non-attachment, and humility; Lao Tzu promises that those who cultivate these things "will have true goodness. Cultivate these in your community, and goodness will catch on. Cultivate these in the World, and goodness will fill the Universe."

NOTES

1   Fox, Matthew, OP. *Meditations with Meister Eckhardt*. Santa Fe: Bear & Co., 1983.

2   Woodruff, Sue. *Meditations with Mechtilde of Magdeburg*. Santa Fe: Bear & Co., 1982.

Festivals of Light

Hanukkah & Christmas

I'd like to start this sermon by talking about rats. Now, I don't mean sewer-dwelling, stinky rats; I'm talking about cute white and hooded rats you find in the pet store, so relax, if you can.

I remember being at the Renaissance Pleasure Faire about twelve years ago with my girlfriend, Cherissa, the woman who was to be my first wife. There, in line, I saw a guy standing there with a live rat on his shoulder. The rat didn't drop off, or run away, or even make a mess. Instead, it rode his shoulder like it was the perch of some imperial transport, going up on two legs now and again to catch a better sniff at the air, now and again scurrying under his hair to try out the air from the other shoulder.

Well, I can tell you, I was entranced. When we got back to her apartment that evening, I told Cherissa, "I want a rat." She said, "You're out of your mind."

I said, "I want a rat." She said, "What you want is a new girl-friend."

I said, "Look, just come down to the pet store with me." That much she would do.

Now, I was not really being fair to Cherissa. I was well aware of the enormous soft spot in Cherissa's heart for animals, and I was playing my cards like a pro. Wouldn't you know it, one look at the baby rats, scurring around, rushing up to sniff us, sleeping in piles and wrestling with each other—Cherissa was hooked. When she finally reached in and picked one up, there were no more complaints about "those scaly tails"; instead, she cooed and rubbed her nose in the soft brown and white fur. "This one is Trevor."

"We have a name," I thought, "*yes!*"

We paid for our rats, and Trevor and Clive came home with us to become our houserats. Well, I couldn't have known it at the time, but the intuition to get rats was one of the best "nudgings" of the Spirit I've ever had, and I'm grateful that I listened to it, because soon, Cherissa and I had married and moved south to the Cal Baptist Campus, where pets were not allowed.

Now, I'm serious about Cherissa's "thing" for animals. It's like heroin: she's got to have her pet fix, and if she doesn't, well, just don't expect to be able to live with her. We wouldn't have been able to hide a dog in our tiny campus apartment, but Clive and Trevor didn't make any noise, and were easily kept out of sight.

They saved Cherissa's life. For the three years we were there, these two rats learned to come when their names were called; they spent their evenings roaming the back of our couch, and secreting little bits of food they scavanged from our television snacking back to a pile in their cage.

Unfortunately, three years is a long time for a rat, and Cherissa and I were both crushed when Trevor came down with a tumor and not to long after, left this world for the great rodent beyond. Clive followed soon after, and though we were in a place where we could have other pets at that time, we were forever touched by these two tiny beasts.

In a time of famine, these little rats became friends and family, they warmed our hearts, and fed our need to care for other beings. In their own tiny way, they made our lives complete, even grand. From these tiny animals came blessings we could not count, could not begin to articulate.

I remembered these two tiny friends when I started to think about this time of year, when the small, even the tiny can be the bearer of great, even magnificent blessings. We're nearing the Winter Solstice, when, although the days are cold and short, they are nonetheless filled with disproportionate joy.

Those of us who are Jews are preparing to celebrate Hanukkah, the Festival of Lights. Jews are quite familiar with the story behind the holiday, but Christians generally are not, and so it is for the benefit of the Christians that I would like to briefly recount this ancient tale.

It starts about a hundred and fifty years before the birth of Jesus, when many Jews were cooperating with Gentile rulers, and were even ready to abolish the practice of Judaism in favor of Greek philosophy. The King even made a law outlawing the Sabbath, kosher foods, and circumcision. The temple at Jerusalem was defiled by pagan worshippers, and used as a place to sacrifice to idols. You can imagine that this did not sit well with those Jews who were loyal to God. One family of faithful believers were from the priestly tribe and were called the Maccabees. Judas Maccabee and his five sons led a revolt, a civil war against the King, and after three years of guerrilla warfare the Maccabees recaptured Jerusalem in spite of the fact that they were grossly outnumbered. Almost immediately they set out to rededicate the temple.

After a new altar had been constructed and everything had been ritually cleansed, the priests found that they had only one bottle of priestly oil. This was a terrible delimma, since one bottle will only burn for one day, and the cleansing requires that the lamp be burned for a full eight days.

Trusting God, and probably hoping to uncover some more oil the next day, they lit the lamp and began their celebration. Unfortunately the next day they were still unable to find more oil; but God didn't seem to care. The story goes that a miracle happened: that one bottle of oil burned for a full eight days, properly consecrating the temple and confirming God's pleasure in their victory. Arthur Waskow says that "the ability of that single jar of oil to stay lit for eight days symbolized how with God's help that tiny amount could unfold into an infinite supply of spiritual riches. Infinite, because the eighth day stood for infinity. Since the whole universe was created in seven days, eight is a symbol of eternity and infinity" (*Seasons*, p. 92).

And so it was that one family and a small band of soldiers were used by God to once again liberate God's people and restore true worship to Israel. At a time when the days were shortest, God chose the small and the insignificant to be lights in the darkness, to shine the way through the gloom, and yes, to change the course of history.

This is no less true for Christians at Christmas, of course. For Christians believe that it was a small and insignificant girl named Mary who was chosen by God to give birth to another great light. This poor and powerless woman, still a teenager, would, by God's will and her own willingness, change the world forever.

Although Jews and Christians may disagree over exactly who Jesus was, I think we can agree on this: Whereas Moses brought the covenant to the Jews, it was through Mary and her child that the covenant came to the gentiles. When Mary and Joseph took their newborn to the Temple for his circumcision, legend has it that the priest there declared that the child was to be "a light unto the gentiles, and the glory of God's people."

So at this time of year, we, Christians and Jews together, celebrate a feast of light. Jews light their little trees, the menorahs, while Christians light their larger Christmas trees. Both testify to a sublime trust in God, to our faith that God is trustworthy, that God is with us, and that God will remain faithful to us, no matter what battles we find we may have to fight.

For it is at this time of year that we see that one little pot of oil, one little band of believers, one willing teenager, one little child, or even one little rat, can be used of God to bring uncountable blessings to the earth.

Christian Heresies in the East

Not long ago, I stood in the pulpit of my church and opened my mouth to begin what everyone expected to be just another sermon. "I have a confession to make," I began, and suddenly everyone was on the edge of their seats. "I am," I continued, "a hhh...heretic."

At this moment, everyone breathed a collective sigh of relief. The mostly elderly, mostly Republican congregation were, I'm sure, terrified that I was going to say "I'm a *homosexual*," but, thank god, I was only a heretic, so that was okay!

Although I grieve that the church I serve was not at that time a place that was openly welcoming of gays and lesbians, I am proud of that fact that they would suffer a sworn heretic to address them from the pulpit a couple of times a month.

Heresy, apparently, is no longer the bad word that it once was, especially in Christian circles. And indeed, why should it be? After all, every religious reformer worth his salt has been branded a heretic sometime in his life. Buddha was a heretic, Jesus was a heretic, Martin Luther was a heretic. Heck, the way I see it, I'm just in good company.

The word heresy, after all, doesn't have such a bad definition, if you consult the dictionary. A heretic is simply "one who questions." Since you are members of the Cultural Integration Fellowship, I would assume that most of you have a critical approach to religion, question things for yourselves, and therefore, perhaps you, too, count yourselves heretics, after a fashion.

For the past two years I have devoted myself to researching and preaching on heresy in the Christian tradition, from the very beginnings of the Christian church to the time of the reformation. In my study I have found not underdogs and losers in the game of religious politics, but instead heroes and saints as yet unsung by the church. Since most of the disputes that caused the heretics of various stripes to be cast out are not only still with us, but widely held by people in the pews as well as the seminaries, it is my hope that we can begin to "welcome home the lost sheep," and to open ourselves to hear, heal, and learn from these fathers and mothers of faith.

This morning I would like to bring you a "Tale of Two Heresies," specifically, the Jewish Christians and the Nestorians. I focus on these two groups not because their heresies are in any way related—they are not—but because these two groups alone made significant missionary efforts in the East, and left a lasting impression on the cultures they touched, long after their numbers and influence had diminished. In their stories, I hope you will find some items of interest, and perhaps even find your own commitment to critical religion encouraged and vivified.

I first met the acquaintance of the Jewish Christians a couple of years ago when I was working on my doctoral dissertation at California Institute of Integral Studies. I was researching early Christian communion practices, and was shocked by what I learned about the earliest of the early churches, the great church at Jerusalem. What I discovered threw me into a spiritual crisis that is still reverberating in my spiritual life. I think one or two of the facts I uncovered may surprise you as well.

If you've ever read the canonical Gospels, it is clear that Jesus' ministry was primarily to the Jewish people, and so, of course, most of his followers were Jews. After Jesus left them they didn't start any new religions. They just kept being Jews. The only thing was, they believed that a new prophet had come to complete and fulfill the Law of Moses. This church was headed by none other than Jesus' flesh and blood brother, James, and included several other members of Jesus' family. The teachings of these earliest of early Christians are remarkable in light of what we have come to think of as Christianity.

First of all, forget the virgin birth. These people were Jesus' own family, and they knew nothing of this story. Instead, they taught that Jesus was an ordinary carpenter until the Christ spirit descended upon him at his baptism, where he was adopted as God's son.

Another surprising revelation is that the Jewish Christians did not believe that Jesus died for anybody's sins. Instead, they taught that he was a prophet the equal or even superior to Moses, who came to wrap up Moses' unfinished business. According to some later writings from this community, they taught that God was a compassionate God who doesn't want any creature to suffer, and hated the practice of animal sacrifice. When Moses led the Israelites out of Egypt, God wanted all sacrifices to end. But Moses pleaded with God, saying, "Hey, this is the only way these people know how to worship. Let's compromise: let them sacrifice, but only to you." God thought this was an acceptable compromise, and in the fullness of time sent the second Moses, Jesus, to complete the deal, to end temple sacrifices altogether. He certainly did not come to be a sacrifice himself, as God finds the sacrifice of any being abhorrent. For the Jewish Christians, Jesus' death was just the inevitable result when someone rocks the boat—and Jesus rocked it big time. Later Jewish Christians even became vegetarians because of their aversion to killing, another way they honored their departed rabbi.

The first real threat to the Jerusalem church came from a pharisaical purist named Saul of Tarsus, who persecuted the Jewish Christians, as he felt they were—surprise—heretics! But later, as Saul himself reports, he fell off his horse on the road to Damascus, hit his head and had a psychedelic vision which he took to be a revelation of the Christ. He became a zealous convert to the new Jewish sect, and appointed himself to be the missionary to the gentiles.

Unfortunately for the Jewish Christians, Paul, as he was called after his conversion, was a creative theologian, and more of a leader than he was a follower of Jesus the Rabbi. He invented an elaborate theology based on Jewish and Greek mysticism as much as on the stories of Jesus. He started preaching his new gospel to Jews in the Diaspora and to gentiles in those lands, where he met with great success.

The Jerusalem Church was horrified. Who was this Paul guy, and why was he teaching all these kooky things about their rabbi? The nerve of this guy!

Paul was talking about Jesus' pre-existence before his birth, about the atoning nature of his death, and that the Jewish Law was optional, or at worst, void.

Paul kept trying to raise money to send to the Jerusalem church to get on their good side and lend his ministry some legitimacy, but this mostly backfired. It finally came to a head in the year 49 CE, when Jesus' brother James conceded to Paul one point: gentile followers of Jesus would not have to be circumcised, but must at least hold to certain aspects of the Law, most of which were forgotten about.

This was a momentous decision, and in retrospect, a tragic one. For from then on, Paul began to wax and the Jewish Christians began to wane.

The felling blow came in the year 70, when the Romans sacked Jerusalem, and the remnants of the Jewish Christians relocated to Syria.

Like most spiritual communities, the relocated Jewish Christians suffered from factionalism. All they seemed to do was multiply and divide. One community went on to become the Ebionites, who became more and more legalistic until they finally died out in the fourth century.

But much longer lived were the St. Thomas Christians, who, after James' death, followed another of Jesus' brothers, Judas Thomas. Also known as "doubting Thomas," Judas Thomas was probably the author of the canonical epistle of Jude, and was the only one of Jesus' brothers who was also an apostle.

But wait, there's more! Not only was Thomas Jesus' brother, but the writings of the Jewish Christians make it very clear that he was Jesus' *twin* brother! Of course that had to be covered up by the Pauline churches, as one could not have a virgin birth if Jesus was born as a twin—unless of course, Thomas was divine, too!

Like other Jewish Christians, the Thomas school of Christianity attached no importance to Jesus' death nor entertained any mythology regarding his miraculous birth. Instead, they focused directly on his teaching, believing that embedded in his koan-like proverbs was the secret of eternal life. Indeed, the Gospel of Thomas starts off by saying that whoever finds the secret to the sayings contained within would never die.

For these Christians, Jesus is simply a teacher who had achieved unitive consciousness and was keenly aware of his union with divinity. Through his teachings he tried to awaken his listeners from their spiritual slumbers and make them likewise aware of their unity with all things. According to them, Jesus did not teach anything about some coming kingdom or imminent apocalypse. Instead, when his disciples asked him when the kingdom would arrive with power, he answered them by saying, "The Kingdom of God is spread out upon the earth, and human beings simply do not see it." He also told them, "Do not listen to those who tell you the Kingdom is in the sky, for then the birds of the air will precede you. Likewise do not pay any attention to those who say it is in the sea, for then the fish will get there before you do. Instead, the Kingdom is inside you *and* it is outside you."

Now this is a great example of Jesus' humor, as no one that I know of ever said that the Kingdom of God was in the ocean, but it also reveals his deeply mystical approach to religion. The Kingdom is in all of us and is all around us. We are surrounded by, filled with, bathed in God. Oneness is the primary theme in the Gospel of Thomas, and much like the Buddha, Jesus did not seem to think that it was something that could be taught, but only experienced by the disciple directly. According to Thomas, the goal for the disciple is to also be Jesus' twin; in other words to gain the unitive consciousness that Jesus enjoyed and thereby also become God's son or daughter.

Now, this sounds so much like Buddhism that we have to ask—how did Jesus know this stuff? Contemporary Bible scholars contend that the Gospel of Thomas is more reliable than any of the canonical Gospels, so this is not a question we can easily dismiss. Did he, as some contend, actually visit India as a child? Probably not, but we do know that there were Buddhist missionaries in Palestine in Jesus' time, so it is not unlikely that Jesus picked up a little Buddha with his regular diet of Moses, leading not only to his own enlightenment, but an amazing new school of Buddhist thought in Jewish guise.

Now the St. Thomas Christians eventually died out in Syria, but inexplicably, they thrived in India. Probably it is because the Thomas school taught doctrines very similar to what was already known in India, and was more easily inculturated than Pauline forms of Christianity.

The Thomas Christians in India, in fact, believe that Thomas himself brought the good news of the Kingdom to their land.

The tale is told that Gundaphorus, king of some province or other of India, wrote to Jesus and asked him to recommend an architect to build his palace.

I wasn't aware—and maybe you weren't either—that Jesus of Nazareth was considered such an expert in exotic architecture that distant kings contacted him for referrals. But that is the tradition, anyway. So Jesus tells his brother to make the journey.

Now this story is not as far-fetched as it sounds. The Mar Thoma Catholic Church in India traces its beginnings all the way back to the very first century, and it is their contention that it was indeed St. Thomas who first brought them the Gospel. Unfortunately not much is known about the early period of this church, since in the twelfth century the Portuguese made the first attempts to colonize India and coerced the Mar Thoma church to comply with Roman Catholic belief and practice, which had previously been completely alien to them. All of their ancient prayer books, sacramentaries, and theological writings were burned by the Portuguese, and today we are left with precious little evidence regarding the origins, theologies, and liturgies of the Mar Thoma Christians; a great loss not only for Christianity, but for historians of religion in general.

The Mar Thoma Christians still proudly proclaim Thomas as their founder, even though their distinctive theology has been denied them.

What a story, huh? The Jewish Christians in general, and the Thomas Christians in particular are an important reminder that it is the victor who gets to write history, and sometimes the real pearls get lost among the sands of time.

The second community I'd like to speak to you about comes later in time and further East in space. The Pauline Christians have earned the favor of the emperor by this time, and are expending a great deal of energy rooting out anyone who disagrees with them. The bishop of Constantinople was Nestorius, an opinionated, tactless, rude, belligerent, and manipulative guy who *really* liked to get his way.

As you might expect, Nestorius' pushiness didn't make him any friends. He didn't care much about this when he was at the height of his power in the middle of the fifth century, as he was a merciless heresy hunter. He defeated the Arians, drove out the Novationists, and decimated the Quartodecimans. But Nestorius did not see that his zeal would come back to bite him in the behind. For the heresy hunter would soon become the hunted.

It was easy to identify the gross heretics, you know, those who said Jesus wasn't human, or that he didn't even have a real body or that he had a *twin*, you know stuff like that. But once those guys have been killed or exiled, the heresy hunters had to look closer and closer to home to find heretics. The teachings defined as heretical became pickier and pickier, and it became harder to actually figure out where they deviated from orthodox teaching. In fact, it almost takes a doctorate in theology to understand in what way Nestorius' teachings could actually be conceived of as heresy. Since we don't all have time or the inclination to do a doctoral program just to understand a subtle theological distinction that none of us cares about anyway, I will attempt to describe Nestorius' "heresy" in a simplistic and grossly inaccurate way in a sentence or two, for your convenience.

Nestorius, like so many heretics before him, was trying to describe exactly how it is that God was in Jesus. According to Nestorius, Jesus shares God's nature because he is God's Son, in the same way as I share human nature because my parents are human. But my parents and I are distinct beings. Nestorius kind of came to the same conclusion about God. God and Christ share the same nature, but they are distinct beings. Nestorius described their union as being similar to the union of a husband and wife. Two distinct beings, made one through a legal covenant.

So even though Nestorius said Jesus and God shared one nature, and were distinct persons, which none of his opponents disagreed with, the language he used implied that these two persons were two distinct beings, which his opponents could not tolerate, since, as the creed says, Jesus is "of one being with the father."

Confused yet? Just think of how theologically sophisticated we are today as compared to folks in the fifth century. Few people were educated at all, and if this distinction is difficult for us to fathom today, imagine trying to explain it to the average person in the street in Nestorius' time.

But it may be that none of this would have come down on Nestorius' head if he had not made so many enemies over "the Mary issue." Ever since the third century, it had been common to refer to Mary as "Theotokos," or the Mother of God. Nestorius thought that this was a logical impossibility, for how could a fifteen-year-old girl give birth to a being older than she is? Nestorius also hated the statues of Mary circulating around, because it smacked to him of idolatry. Especially since it seemed that the statues were virtually identical to the statues of Isis and her baby son Horus, which had been popular for centuries. Folks just baptized their idols in Christian garb and kept right on worshipping them, and Nestorius wasn't going to stand for it.

Well, our poor bishop of Constantinople lost that round, and he lost the next one as well, since he was condemned in the year 431. Nestorius was exiled to Egypt, where he died in poverty and obscurity twenty years later in 451.

But that is not the end of the story, of course, or we wouldn't be talking about poor disagreeable Nestorius today. Being the bishop of Constantinople is a *big* deal, kind of like being the pope of the East. Nestorius had a *lot* of bishops that agreed with his ideas, and when the council that condemned both them and Nestorius was over, though some of the bishops that sided with him recanted and were received back into "God's good graces," the bishops in Persia continued to stay true to Nestorius' formulation.

The Christians of Persia lived as a minority religion in a country that was predominately Zoroastrian. Zoroastrianism is often thought of as a dualistic religion that teaches that there are two gods in the universe, a god of goodness and light, and a god of evil and darkness, and that these two gods are in a constant battle over the fate of the earth. The wise men who came to visit the baby Jesus were thought to be Zoroastrian priests, even by the Zoroastrians themselves. For when the Persians conquered the Holy Land in the early seventh century, they destroyed every church and shrine in Israel except for one: the Church of the Nativity in Bethlehem, where, not coincidentally, a mosaic of the three wise Zoroastrian sages was set over the door.

The effect that being Christians in a non-Christian country had on the Nestorians is that they were allowed to inculturate their religion to a far greater degree, now that the churches of the Roman empire were minding their own business. They really got the hang of translating their Christian faith into the idioms and traditions of the lands they happened to be living in, and this was a great boon to them in their strenuous missionary efforts in the seventh through ninth centuries.

Since the West was Orthodox, the Nestorians turned towards the East. A missionary named Alopen was sent to evangelize China. Amazingly, Alopen was welcomed into the court of the Chinese emperor, who listened to Alopen with great interest. After all, to the Chinese, the West is the spiritual direction, so any spiritual teachers to come from the West, such as Buddha, and now Alopen, were given a good hearing, at least under the emperor Cheng-kuan. The emperor was so impressed with what came to be called "the shining teaching," that he ordered the Christian Sutras, or scriptures, to be translated immediately into Chinese.

And boy, did Alopen translate! Quickly getting the hang of things in the East, the scriptures and other writings that Alopen translated were replete with Taoist and Buddhist imagery. In Alopen's works, Jesus doesn't come to die for our sins, but to bring the great raft to rescue all beings from the suffering sin causes. Alopen had a genius for inculturating the gospel, for making the core teachings of Christianity understandable in the symbols and imagery of the country he was in. So successful was Alopen that soon there were Nestorian churches and monasteries in every province of China.

Unfortunately, not all of the emperors were so magnanimous or tolerant, and in the ninth century, all "foreign" religions, including Buddhism and Christianity, were outlawed. The churches were closed, and over three thousand Nestorian monks were returned to regular life. Most of the monuments were destroyed, but some Nestorian crosses and one very significant artifact, the Nestorian Stone, still survive, along with many of Alopen's Sutras.

The Mongols to the North were among the various Chinese peoples evangelized, and history tells us that even Genghis Khan's mother was a Nestorian Christian, along with many of his officers and soldiers. Christianity survived among the Mongols much longer than in the rest of China; even as late as the thirteenth century two Mongolian priests set out from the cathedral in Peking with the blessing of Kublai Kahn. They visited Constantinople and Rome and even celebrated communion in the court of Edward I in England.

Thus it was that this tiny pocket of heretics from Persia became one of the greatest missionary forces the world has ever known, and introduced to all of the East a form of Christianity that fit their culture, made sense to them, and continues to speak even today to those willing to do the research. Though most of the Nestorians in Persia were forcibly converted to Islam, there are still Nestorian churches in the East, some of whom have, ironically, kissed and made up with the Orthodox, realizing after fifteen hundred years that their squabbles were pretty petty to begin with.

History is full of such ironies, but I have yet to tell you about the tastiest irony of all, and a most appropriate one at this holiday time when the image of the Madonna and child can be found even on a postage stamp. It seems that before the Nestorians arrived in China, a minor deity of compassion was widely worshipped. His name was Quan-Yin, and the missionaries would have encountered countless shrines to this deity on their journeys. But human nature is hard to shake, you know, and even though Nestorius hated the little statues of the Virgin Mary, his own monks still clung to them, and carried them with them into China.

Isn't it odd, then, that after only a couple hundred years, Quan-Yin, deity of compassion, came to be known as a female deity, rather than male, and amazingly, her later statues showed her cradling a child in her lap, almost identical to Isis and Horus, or Mary and Jesus. Quan-Yin is still a popular figure even today. In fact, rarely a week goes by that I don't see a statue of her right here in the Bay Area.

Funny how these things come around, isn't it? So what is it we can learn from the Nestorians? First, perhaps, do unto others as you would have them do unto you. If Nestorius had followed that simple scriptural admonition, his end may have been much different indeed. But a much more positive lesson comes to us from his followers, who understood that the good news of the Enlightened One can be translated into any language, any culture. Unlike Western missionaries, who reviled the local cultures and insisted that converts become experts in Western philosophy and theology, the Nestorians showed us the kind of power that good news can have when it is allowed to be spoken in people's native tongues.

Although these two communities—the Jewish Christians and the Nestorians—have largely been lost to obscurity, a little digging can be richly rewarding, for it reveals to us that the form of Christianity that has come down to us is not the only game in town. It is not the oldest form of Christian belief nor the most scholastically reliable. What the Jewish Christians and the Nestorians reveal to us is that the message of Jesus is one of uniting, not dividing. It is an inclusive message that has the power to reach across cultural divides and enlighten all peoples. It is a universal message of hope that can stand strong alongside the teachings of Buddha or Ramanuja, and indeed, we find that these supposedly disparate teachings are in amazing harmony. This is the gift that the Jewish Christians and the Nestorians have for us this Christmastide: the unity of all things is not the exclusive property of any sectarian teaching, but is the spiritual heritage of all people of faith, now and forever.

I would like to close with a reading from "The Sutra Which Aims at Mysterious Rest and Joy," an anonymous Chinese Nestorian document from the eighth century. It presents a parable, supposedly told by Jesus, which I had never heard before. If you would like to close your eyes and get comfortable, imagine yourself on the shore of the Sea of Galilee. Strangely, Simon Peter and Jesus are dressed as Chinese Buddhist monks, but don't let that deter you. Jesus turns to Peter and, according to this Sutra, he says:

> The teachings can be compared to the Precious Mountain. Its jade forests and pearl fruits, translucent and shining, sweet tasting and beautifully perfumed, can cure a person of hunger and thirst and heal all ills.
>
> There was a sick man who heard of this mountain. Day and night he longed to reach this mountain and the thought never left him.
>
> But, sadly, the way was far and the mountain very high and steep. The sick man was also a hunchback and was too feeble to climb such

a mountain. In vain did he try to fulfil his dream. He simply could not undertake it. But he had a near relation who was both wise and sincere. This man set up scaling ladders and had steps cut into the mountain and with others he pushed and pulled the sick man up the mountain until he reached the summit. Immediately, the sick man's illness was cured.

Know this, Simon Peter, that the people coming to this mountain of true teachings were for a long time confused and in misery because they were burdened by their worldly passions. They had heard of the truth and knew it could lead them to the Way of Rest and Joy—to the Mountain of Rest and Joy. They tried to reach the mountain and to scale it, but in vain, for love and faith had almost died within them.

Thereupon, the Almighty Lord made himself known. He came as the near relative of the people and taught them with such skill and sincerity that they understood that he was both the scaling ladder and the stone steps by means of which they could understand the True Way and rid themselves of their burdens of confusion forever.

—from *The Jesus Sutras,* translated by Martin Palmer

(Wellspring/Ballentine, 2001).

False Self
and Original Nature

Reflections from Suzuki and Merton

"Evidently," D.T. Suzuki writes, "Zen is the most irrational, inconceivable thing in the world."[1] This is a common response amongst those investigating Zen, or Ch'an, Buddhism for the first time. It is baffling because it evades logical explanation, and in fact often avoids any explanation at all. One of the most baffling aspects that the newcomer encounters is the assertion that we are not who we think we are. We are not the person we have been brought up to believe ourselves to be, and our delusion is the source of most of our troubles. Zen is a process that reveals to us who we really are, and calls our real identity our "Original Nature."

Thomas Merton, who derived his philosophy from both Western and Eastern sources, called the self we think ourselves to be our "false self." As in Zen, the spiritual journey, for Merton, is the quest for the Original Nature, or as Merton calls it, the True Self. For Merton, "the self that begins the journey is not the self that arrives.[2]

Just what is this elusive Original Nature or True Self, and how does it differ from the False Self? In this paper we shall take a look at both, and also comment on how to make the journey from one to the other.

167

A Buddhist fable is told of a small fish that hears a tale about the ocean, which sounds like a wonderful place, indeed. Immediately, he sets out to find this place. He swims far and wide and cannot find any sign of this thing called "ocean." Finally, he meets a wise old fish who tells him that he is already swimming in the ocean, that he need search no longer. The little fish is overcome, and swims away, enlightened.[3] This is a tale of the True Self. We, like the little fish, believe that the Ocean, that Life, that God is somewhere "out there." The truth is that we are swimming in God, and we never even knew it. We are not separate, we are not cut off, we do not need to look for anything.

In Zen teaching, the idea that we are separate creatures is an illusion, and the ego that we have built up for ourselves, this "I" with which we refer to ourselves, is also an illusion. Merton agrees, and says that "when the...identity of the ego is taken to be my deepest and only identity, when I am thought to be nothing but the sum total of all my relationships, when I cling to this self and make it the center around which and for which I live, I then make my empirical identity into the False Self. My own self then becomes the obstacle to realizing my true self."[4]

In clinging to this illusion, we perpetuate the suffering that plagues us. We know that something is very wrong, and we scramble to fill the void we instinctively feel inside us in the only way we know how. We have been well-trained as consumers, and our addictive rush towards anything that will pacify us, however temporarily, reveals the depths of our individual and cultural bondage. "We live in a shadow existence," writes James Finley, "in which we find ourselves between ourselves and God. As helpless observers, we watch ourselves living out a life we know to be a fragmented tragedy."[5] The False Self is itself this fragmentation, the very thing that cuts us off from wholeness.

The Zen practitioner realizes that the ego-self is, in Merton's words, "not final or absolute; it is a provisional self-construction which exists, for practical purposes, only in a sphere of relativity. Its existence has meaning in so far as it does not become fixated or centered upon itself as ultimate."[6]

Of course, once we begin to realize some of this, the ego invariably feels threatened (with good reason!) and switches into survival mode, fighting with everything it has for its continued sovereignty, sometimes causing "spiritual emergencies" and psychotic episodes that are really "spiritual *emergences*." According to Merton, the False Self "fears and recoils from what is beyond it and above it. It dreads the alluring emptiness and darkness of the interior self."[7] Even so, the ego may play along for a while, and allow us our forays into meditation and spirituality, allowing it to be stretched almost to the vanishing point. But so long as it can "snap back" and regain control once the meditation period ends, we are still acting out of the False Self.

"As long as there is an 'I' that is the definite subject of a contemplative experience," writes Merton, "an 'I' that is aware of itself and its contemplation, an 'I' that can possess a certain 'degree of spirituality,' then we have not yet passed over the Red Sea, we have not yet 'gone out of Egypt.' We remain in the realm of multiplicity, activity, incompleteness, striving, and desire."[8]

When the False Self begins to realize its unreality, then, according to Finley, "it begins to convince itself that it is what it does. Hence, the more it does, achieves and experiences, the more real it becomes."[9] Unfortunately, this is a futile effort, and in its insecurity, in trying to prove its efficacy in the world, the False Self can drive a person to exhaustion or madness. Suzuki says, "If you want to seek the Buddha, you ought to see into your own Nature, which is the Buddha himself. The Buddha is a free man—a man who neither works nor achieves. If, instead...you turn away and seek the Buddha in external things, you will never get at him."[10] The great Ch'an master Hui-neng agrees, saying, "the deluded mind looks outside itself to seek the Buddha, not yet realizing that its own self-nature is Buddha."[11]

Eventually, the seeker must realize that "the nothingness he fears is in fact the treasure he longs for."[12] Merton says that,

> The only full and authentic purification is that which turns a man completely inside out, so that he no longer has a self to defend, no longer an intimate heritage to protect against...the full maturity of the spiritual life cannot be reached unless we first pass through the dread, anguish, trouble, and fear that necessarily

accompany the inner crisis of "spiritual death" in which we finally abandon our attachment to our exterior self and surrender completely...."[13]

This is the purpose of Zen practice, then: to bring us to this
point. It may seem a lonely and desolate point indeed, but it is
only in this sort of death that the True Self may be born in our
consciousness. On the eve of writing this paper I had a dream. In
it, I had been condemned to death by burning. All of us who were
condemned were together in a classroom receiving instruction
from a cheery man on how to die. We were told that it would not
be painful and that we would have the best seats in the house!
What was most curious, though, was that we would die in neat
rows, sitting in a zazen position. I was scared, of course, but the
instructor was very comforting. Perhaps it would not be so bad
after all, I thought. After I awoke I realized what a meaningful
dream it was. Zen is about death. The death of the False Self; the
extinguishing of the ego and the birth of our true knowing. As
Jesus says, "He who loses his life, shall find it."

Merton uses similarly macabre imagery when he says that,

> Zen enriches no one. There is no body to be found. The birds
> may come and circle for a while in the place where it is thought to
> be. But they soon go elsewhere. When they are gone, the "noth-
> ing," the "no-body" that was there, suddenly appears. That is Zen.
> It was there all the time but the scavengers missed it, because it
> was not their kind of prey.[14]

Let us now endeavor to discover the "no-body" who is always
there. In a famous Zen story, Ming once asked Hui-neng what
Ch'an was. Hui-neng did not answer this question directly.
Instead, he replied "Show me your original face, as it was before
you were born." Ming was instantly enlightened.[15]

This enlightenment was the result of Ming's sudden realization
of his True Self, his "original face." Zen has many words for this
same concept. "Original Nature," "Self-Nature," and "Suchness"
are a few of the more familiar. In Chinese, according to Therese
Peng, "self-nature" is composed of two characters, "tze" and
"hsing." "Tze" means "self," or "one's own," and "hsing" means
"innate," "uncreated," or "spirit." "Thus," writes Peng, "'self-

nature' implies one's innate nature or spiritual nature, one's original nature."[16]

One's "original nature" is not grounded in our ego; it does not depend on anything we do. It is about who we are. It is not about our little "self" which the False Self is so interested in, but about our big "Self," our identity with the cosmos, with God. Merton writes,

> Let us remind ourselves that another, metaphysical, consciousness is still available to [us]. It starts not from the thinking and self-aware subject but from Being, ontologically seen to be beyond and prior to the subject-object division. Underlying the subjective experience of the individual self there is an experience of Being. This is totally different from an experience of self-consciousness. It is completely non-objective. It has in it none of the split and alienation that occurs when the subject becomes aware of itself as a quasi-object. The consciousness of Being...is an immediate experience that goes beyond reflexive awareness. It is not "consciousness of" but pure consciousness, in which the subject as such "disappears."[17]

Our True Self is not distinct, then, from the rest of reality. Who we are *is what is*. And what is, is God; or as our Zen friends would say, Buddha. In the ancient Zen writing, *The Record of the Transmission of the Lamp*, Tao-hsin explains it thusly,

> The immeasurable subtle virtues are in the source of mind. All the doors of precept, meditation, wisdom, spiritual penetration, and transformation are contained in one's mind and will not separate from the mind. All obstructions of defilements and karmas of worry and trouble, are, in origin, empty. All causes and effects are dreams and illusions. There are no three realms from which we can leave and no Bodhi for which we can seek. The inner natures and forms of man and no-man are equal. The great Way is empty and vast. It is beyond thought and deliberation. You, at this instant, have this Dharma and are without lack. You are no different from Buddha....Whether you walk or stay, sit or lie down, and whatever you see or meet, all are the subtle functions of Buddha. It is joy without sorrow. This is called Buddha.[18]

There is nothing but Buddha. In the Mahayana Buddhist tradition, Buddha is often seen as a personification of reality.[19] There is nothing but Buddha, nothing but God, and once our identity is rooted in him, then our True Self can emerge. Merton says, "since our inmost 'I' is the perfect image of God, then when that 'I' awakens, he finds within himself the Presence of Him Whose image he is. And, by a paradox beyond all human expression, God and the soul seem to have but one single 'I'."[20]

Finley explains:

> Our union with God is our person, it is who we are and not any thing we know. It is precisely our identity that emerges once we are freed by death from all the things we thought ourselves to be. Therefore, nothing can be said that, by the sheer informational content of the statement, could bring about awareness of our identity-giving relationship with the living God.
>
> Purely objective statements miss the mark, for God is not an object. He is Person. Nor are we, as persons, objects. Here all is Subject. There is no "object" "out there" to "see." Here all is presence and communion. Here everything, including our own individuality, remains itself—or, rather, for the first time becomes itself, but does so only by opening out into the oneness that is God.[21]

But paradoxically, although this sounds very transcendent and metaphysical, this participation in Being is, in Zen's phrase, "nothing special." Things simply are what they are. And their natural simplicity—including our natural simplicity—is precisely what is so divine. "The proper harmony of the universe is realized" says Alan Watts, "when each 'thing-event' is allowed to be freely and spontaneously itself, without interference.... Do not separate yourself from the world and try to order it around."[22]

This is a very different approach, of course, from the strategy of the False Self, which is to take command and force reality into a shape that pleases it. The True Self is just what it is—just what is—and needs no prodding or shaping. It is not dependent upon accomplishment, upon "righteousness," upon social stature for its esteem. "True Self esteem" comes from "my knowledge of myself in silence," as Merton says, "not by reflection on my self, but by penetration to the mystery of my true self which is beyond words and concepts...[which] opens out into the silence and the 'subjectivity' of God's own self."[23]

This "is-ness" is often called "suchness" in Buddhist writings. As the Bodhisattva Manjusri says in the *Saptasatika*,

> Suchness neither becomes nor ceases to become; thus do I see the Buddha. Suchness does not stand at any point or place; thus do I see the Buddha. Suchness is neither past, future, nor present; thus do I see the Buddha. Suchness does not arise from the dual or the non-dual; thus do I see the Buddha. Suchness is neither impure nor pure; thus do I see the Buddha. Suchness neither arises nor comes to an end; thus do I see the Buddha."[24]

Simply living in the now, living the moment in simplicity is to live the life of God. This is the life in which our True Self can begin to emerge. Merton says that the True Self "is like a very shy wild animal that never appears at all whenever an alien presence is at hand, and comes out only when all is peaceful, in silence, when he is untroubled and alone. He cannot be lured by anyone or anything, because he responds to no lure except that of the divine freedom."[25]

When the True Self emerges and begins to live through us—for the False Self must, if this is to happen, relinquish its control—it is not our life, but "Christ's life.... When you eat breakfast, Christ is eating breakfast. When you go to work, Christ is going to work. When you meet your brother...Christ is meeting Christ."[26] Eventually, it is possible to live a life that is "God living in God and identifying a created life with His own Life so that there is nothing left of any significance but God living in God."[27]

The paradox is that there is little we can "do" to achieve this consciousness. As Watts says, "since one's own True Nature is already the Buddha nature, one does not have to do anything to make it so. On the contrary, to seek to become Buddha is to deny that one is already Buddha—and this is the sole basis upon which Buddhahood can be realized!"[28] There are, nonetheless, some methods which Zen masters, and Christian mystics have devised which can help.

In another Zen story, Chao-chou asked Nan-chuan,

> "What is the Way?" Nan-chuan answered, "The ordinary mind is the Way." Chao-chou asked, "Please tell me which direction to approach it." Nan-chuan answered, "If there is any direction, it is the wrong way." Chao-chou asked, If there is no direction, how

can it be called the Way?" Nan-chuan answered, "The Way belongs neither to knowing nor to no-knowing. Knowing is a false feeling. No-knowing is no feeling. If the real Way is achieved, it is like the supreme space which is empty and boundless. How can it be named right or wrong?"[29]

As in Taoism, the way ahead is not to "do" something, but instead, "not-doing." The seventh century Ch'an master Fa-yung said, "All talk has nothing to do with one's Original Nature, which can only be reached through sunyata. "No-thought" is the Absolute Reality, in which the mind ceases to act. When one is free from thoughts, one's nature has reached the Absolute.... The nature of Reality is invisible and cannot be understood by our conscious mind."[30]

Traditionally this is achieved by meditation. There is much debate, however, over the proper way to meditate. Some methods, popular in both the East and the West, involve concentration on a word, an image or an idea. This is called catophatic meditation by Christian mystics.

Another way, most popular in Zen practice, is to make the mind empty of all thought. This is called apophatic meditation and is advocated by many Zen and Ch'an schools, including the Renzai school. Achieving this "emptiness is not so easy, though," Alan Watts writes. "The true mind is "no-mind," which is to say that it is not to be regarded as an object of thought or action, as if it were a thing to be grasped and controlled. The attempt to work on one's own mind is a vicious circle."[31] One way some Zen schools have approached this problem is simply not to try, as in the method known as "just sitting," practiced by the Soto school. With this method, one does not try to empty the mind, nor fix it on any object, but simply to sit and note what arises, immediately letting it go. The goal here is not emptiness, but mindfulness. Eventually, if one is successful, the mind will quiet of its own accord, without striving. Hui-neng said, "Our Self-Nature is at root clear and quiet. You have but to use this mind to directly become a Buddha."[32]

Having meditation as a base from which to begin our journey to our True Self, we must be careful lest we put ourselves in danger of becoming too transcendent, too "other-worldly," too far removed from ordinary life. Zen insists that Buddhahood is not found in spiritual extravagances, but only in ordinary, everyday experience. It is, as we noted above, "nothing special." Suzuki says, "Salvation must be sought in the finite itself, there is nothing infinite apart from finite things; if you seek something transcendental, that will cut you off from this world of relativity, which is the same thing as the annihilation of yourself. You do not want salvation at the cost of your own experience."[33]

Our way forward begins exactly where we are, not in some monastery, not in some arcane or exotic practice, but in getting up and shaving, going to work, cooking dinner, taking out the trash. We need to begin to view all our experience as spiritual practice. A bumper sticker I saw recently said, "How you do anything is how you do everything." Just living is a meditative practice, if we attempt to live mindfully, and aren't trying to be something or someone we're not—haven't we had enough of "False Selves," after all?

Thomas Merton once preached a sermon to some birds, saying, "Esteemed friends, birds of noble lineage, I have no message to you except this: be what you are: be birds. Thus you will be your own sermon to yourselves!"[34]

"The Ultimate standpoint of Zen," says Suzuki, "is that we have been led astray through ignorance.... [We] find a split in our own being, that there was from the very beginning no need for a struggle between the finite and the infinite, that the peace we are seeking so eagerly after has been there all the time."[35] The prescription for discovering the True Self, therefore, is simple: be observant (pray or meditate) and be yourself. Nothing else is required. Anything else will be counterproductive. As Finley says, in describing our journey towards God, "Where must we go to see him?—Nowhere! What can we do to have him? Nothing! All we can do, at least for a moment (an eternal moment) is to abandon all doing and be who we are in him, and open ourselves to his life within us. It is then we will at once see him and ourselves."[36]

Suzuki call this "returning to one's home." He says, "You have now found yourself; from the very beginning nothing has been kept away from you. It was yourself that closed the eye to the face. In Zen there is nothing to explain, nothing to teach, that will add to your knowledge. Unless it grows out of yourself, no knowledge is really of value to you."[37]

It is clear that Suzuki and Merton have much to teach us. From their perspectives, Zen and Christian contemplation, we get stereoscopic views of a universal human condition, the preoccupation with a pretender, the False Self. But we also have hope of discovering who we really are, our Original Nature, our True Self. The way ahead is not easy; it is elusive and perplexing, and mindfulness and sincerity are not instantly perfectible skills. We must be kind to ourselves, and in this way honor ourselves and our paths.

Hsin-hsin Ming offers us a poem filled with sage advice:

> Follow your nature and accord with the Tao;
> saunter along and stop worrying.
> If your thoughts are tied you spoil what is genuine....
> Don't be antagonistic to the world of the senses,
> for when you are not antagonistic to it,
> it turns out to be the same as complete Awakening.
> The wise person does not strive;
> the ignorant man ties himself up....
> If you work on your mind with your mind,
> how can you avoid an immense confusion?[38]

NOTES

1. Suzuki, D.T. *Zen Buddhism* (New York: Doubleday, 1956), p. 13.

2. Finley, James. *Merton's Palace of Nowhere* (Notre Dame: Ave Maria Press,1978), p. 17.

3. Peng, Therese. *Meditation and Psycho-Spiritual Transformation* (Doctoral Dissertation, CIIS, 1993), p. 1.

4. Finley, 18.

5. *Ibid.*, 38.

6. Merton, Thomas. *Zen and the Birds of Appetite* (New York: New Directions, 1968), p. 26.

7. Finley, 101.

8. *Ibid.*, 130.

9. *Ibid.*, 35.

10. Suzuki, 88.

11. Peng, 40.

12. Finley, 111.

13. *Zen and the Birds...*, 24.

14. *Ibid.*, 9.

15. Peng, 44.

16. *Ibid.*, 34.

17. *Zen and the Birds...*, 23-24.

18. Wu, Yi. *The Mind of Chinese Ch'an* (San Francisco: Great Learning, 1989), p. 18-19.

19. Watts, Alan. *The Way of Zen* (New York: Pantheon, 1957), p. 68.

20. Finley, 87.

21. *Ibid.*, 124.

22. Watts, 71.

23. Merton, Thomas. *Thoughts in Solitude* (New York: Farrar, Straus and Cudahy, 1956), p. 70.

24. Watts. 68.

25. Finley, 91.

26. *Ibid.*, 72.

27. Merton, Thomas. *New Seeds of Contemplation* (New York: Harcourt, Brace and Co., 1953), p. 284.

28. Watts, 69.

29. Wu, 85.

30. Peng, 38.

31. Watts, 93.

32. Peng, 1.

33. Suzuki, 14.

34. Finley, 108.

35. Suzuki, 13.

36. Finley, 112.

37. Suzuki, 97.

38. Watts, 89.

Process Thought
and the Hopi Universe

Wisdom comes at us from all directions. Just as, with the discovery that "curved space" traveling in one direction will eventually bring one back full circle to where the journey was begun, so it is that the linear, Cartesian, parts-mentality stream of Western thought eventually brings us back to where we began: the perception and appreciation of the whole. This return to holistic awareness in philosophy, religion, and science not only revolutionizes and energizes these fields, but it humbles us that it has taken us so long to discover what so-called "primitive peoples" have known so well for so long: all things are interconnected. It humbles us, and in so doing, enables us to admit that perhaps many of our perceptions of the universe are just that, perceptions, and not necessarily "objective" reality at all.

In reviewing certain perceptions of time and the nature of the universe as perceived by the Hopi peoples of North America, it became apparent that many of them are quite similar to the cosmological intuitions of early twentieth-century philosopher Alfred North Whitehead. Following the lead of Hegel in the Western philosophical tradition, Whitehead came to many conclusions regarding God, the universe, and the nature of time and its relationship to reality that are strikingly similar to the Hopi cosmology. In the following pages we will examine some of Whitehead's ideas and describe their similarities to Native American thinking, especially as described in Benjamin Whorf's article "An American Indian Model of the Universe."

Both philosophies share a common intuition: that the material universe is not distinguishable from the progress of matter through time. Static, objective matter is an illusion of the Western imagination. The reality is harder to pin down, messier, and far more glorious. Matter and time cannot be divorced, and we can only talk about one in terms of the other. In Whitehead's view, there are no static moments, all is moving in four dimensions at all times; all is in flux; all is in the process of changing from one state to another; all is in the process of "becoming" other than it is. There is no choice: time marches relentlessly onward, and any illusions of permanence or security are just that, illusions. All of reality is in a constant state of "becoming," in process toward the fulfillments of its potentialities. Likewise, as Suzuki and Knudtson write, "the Native Mind tends to view the universe as the dynamic interplay of elusive and ever-changing natural forces, not as a vast array of static physical objects. It tends to see the entire natural world as somehow alive and animated by a single, unifying life force, whatever its local Native name. It does not reduce the universe to progressively smaller conceptual bits and pieces."[1]

In both philosophies, separating the Creator from the Creation is impossible, and even distinguishing them is sometimes a challenge. As Roger Sperry, the Nobel Prize-winning neurobiologist says, "The Creator and Creation cannot be separated. The two of necessity become intimately interfused and evolve together in a relation of mutual interdependence. Thus, what destroys, degrades, or enhances one does the same to the other."[2] In a Hopi creation myth, the androgynous being A'wonawil'ona created clouds and the waters from his/her own breath. "He-She is the blue vault of the firmament. The breath clouds of the gods are tinted with the yellow of the north, the blue-green of the west, the red of the south, and the silver of the east of A'wonawil'ona; they are himself, as he is the air itself; and when the air takes on the form of a bird it is but a part of himself. Through the light, clouds, and air he becomes the essence and creator of vegetation."[3] In a similar Navajo myth, Changing Woman fashions the Navajo people from shreds of her own skin.[4] In both of these stories the natural world is not separate from the Creator, but part of the Creator him/herself.

In Whitehead's (and Hegel's) philosophy, God and the universe are a single organism. In a way, the universe is the "body" of God. As Meister Eckhart puts it, "God created all things in such a way that they are not outside himself."[5] Everything that is, then, is in God. From such a perspective, nothing that exists in the phenomenal world may be considered in and of itself, but only as it relates to the Whole, the Absolute. That the part is a separate entity is an illusion, only the Whole is real.[6] Hegel himself sums it up: "Philosophy is concerned with the true and the true is the whole."[7] But, so far as Whitehead is concerned, it is not just the universe that is dependent upon God for existence. His God is more reciprocal and limited than we are used to thinking of God in the West. For Whitehead, God is intricately bound up in the progress of the universe, and is dependent upon it for his/her own growth. Whitehead, therefore, claims that "it is as true to say that God creates the world as that the world creates God."[8]

The Native American conception of deity likewise differs from the prevalent Western notion. As David Suzuki and Peter Knudtson write, "Native wisdom sees spirit, however one defines that term, as dispersed throughout the cosmos or embodied in an inclusive, cosmos-sanctifying divine being. Spirit is not concentrated in a single monotheistic Supreme Being."[9] The Native God, like Whitehead's, is not a static one. It is a deity caught up in the ebb and flow of the material universe. God is not a thing with an objective, separate existence, but is as much a process as anything else in existence. Since this has been the Native view for some time, it is no wonder that Native Americans have had such a hard time describing their conception of God to White People. As Dan Moonhawk Alford writes, "The toughest job the Indians ever faced was explaining to the white man who their God was. That's because they don't have a Noun-God...you can't make it into a person with form and shape. It's not a person, but a process—a profound mysteriousing."[10]

This view of God and the universe is, for the Native American, hard-wired into their language system. Native languages, says Alford, "are more verby, come out of a worldview which pays primary attention to process, relationships, rhythms, vibrations, and change—where only flux is constant and can be counted upon."[11] For Whitehead, then, trying to describe his "new" view of the universe, language was, understandably, a problem of profound proportions. There are simply no words in the English language to describe Whitehead's ideas. Thus, he had to set about creating some. This was still problematic, since he was trying to describe a universe that was process-oriented—verb-oriented—in the context of a matter-bound—noun-based—language system. This makes Whitehead tough reading regardless of one's reading skills. He could well have benefited from being able to explore his ideas in a language like Hopi, which is ideally suited to such an endeavor.

Both Whitehead and the Hopi divide the universe into two qualities of being, the manifest and the unmanifest. According to Benjamin Whorf, for the Hopi the manifest, or the "objective," comprises "all that is or has been accessible to the senses, the historical physical universe, in fact, with no attempt to distinguish between present and past, but excluding everything that we call the future."[12] Whitehead refers to all things manifest as "occasions," or "actual occasions." These are the basic units, the "drops of experience," the "final real things of which the world is made, and there is no going behind them to find anything more real."[13] Everything that is is an actual occasion, from an amoeba to God. Everything that can be experienced is an ongoing string of experiences unto itself, and is itself an occasion, a moment that actually exists within a certain span of time. Only things that can be measured in time have any existence. Apart from temporal existence, there is nothing. Thus, an "occasion" is a thing that exists within time, be it a rock or the Horsehead Nebula.

The other pole of being, the unmanifest, is called the "subjective" by Whorf in reference to the Hopi conception of the universe. The subjective, says Whorf, "Comprises all that we call future, but not merely this; it includes equally and indistinguishably all that we call mental—everything that appears or exists in the mind, or, as the Hopi would prefer to say, in the heart, not only the heart of man, but the heart of animals, plants, and things, and behind and within all the forms and appearances of nature in the heart of nature, and by an implication and extension...in the heart of the Cosmos, itself."[14] Further, the subjective contains "all mentality, intellection, and emotion, the essence and typical form of which is the striving of purposeful desire, intelligent in character, toward manifestation."[15] The subjective is "the realm of expectancy, of desire and purpose, of vitalizing life, of efficient causes, of thought thinking itself out from an inner realm into manifestation. It is in a dynamic state, yet not a state of motion—it is not advancing toward us out of a future, but already with us in vital and mental form, and its dynamism is at work in the field of eventuation or manifesting, i.e. evolving without motion from the subjective by degrees to a result which is the objective."[16]

For Whitehead, it is in the realm of the subjective that there exists "unmanifest objects." These are known as "eternal objects," and can be thought of as eternal archetypes that are true apart from material existence. And, like the Hopi view, it is this realm, the unmanifest, that gives what is manifest its shape. Whitehead writes, "The things which are temporal [actual occasions] arise by their participation in the things which are eternal [eternal objects]. The two sets are mediated by a thing which combines the actuality of what is temporal with the timelessness of what is potential. This final entity is the divine element in the world, by which the barren inefficient disjunction of abstract potentialities obtains primordially the efficient conjunction of ideal realization."[17]

What Whitehead is saying (in his own impenetrable fashion) is that actual occasions are determined by what is, they exist in the now. But in the realm of the eternal objects lies the infinite potential of what might be. According to Whitehead, eternal objects have their existence in the mind of God, because s/he, having absolute union with the material plane, is integral in every occasion of becoming. Whitehead writes, "Apart from such orderings, there would be a complete disjunction of eternal objects unrealized in the temporal world."[18] God, then, is the mediator, the interface between the conceptual potentiality and the material reality. Yet Whitehead's God is not the only occasion with a will, for every occasion has some sort of need for satisfaction which Whitehead terms "subjective aim." All beings, then, participate in giving birth to the manifest.

Two concepts that are key for Whitehead are "prehension" and "concrescence." Prehension refers to an entity's interactions, interrelations in time with its environment. "Prehension" sounds like the word "apprehension," yet, as William S. Sahakian describes it, "subjects are the [actual] occasions... their objects are the data [from its environment]; and prehension provides the relationship between them." Prehension is "incognitive apprehension; it involves more than mere perception but lacks the cognitive element."[19] A subject "prehends" an object by its experience with the object. If the object changes the subject in some way, it is called a "positive prehension;" if the subject remains unchanged (except for the addition of the encounter) it is called a "negative prehension." Thus, positive prehensions effect what the subject is to become.[20]

"Concrescence" is analogous to the Buddhist concept of "dependent co-arising," in that a multiplicity of subjects interrelate in such a way that a more complex unity results. Actual entities "concresce" into larger entities. Whitehead writes, "Each instance of concrescence is itself the novel individual 'thing' in question. There are not 'the concrescence' and the 'novel thing'; when we analyse the novel thing we find nothing but the concrescence. 'Actuality' means nothing else than this ultimate entry into the concrete, in abstraction from which there is mere nonentity."[21]

These ideas are central to Whitehead's thought, and yet our ability to grasp and utilize such "action-bound" concepts is sorely limited by our language, which has no precedent for such a train of thought. It is simply the wrong tool for the job. The Hopi language, though, is ideally suited to such description. Hopi has verb forms which perfectly describe the very edge of "becoming." They would certainly have been helpful to Whitehead in describing the above processes. For the eternal object which is about to become manifest through an impending prehension or concrescence, the expective tense may be used. The expective is "that which is beginning to emerge into manifestation...the nearer edge of the subjective cuts across and includes a part of our present time, *viz.* the moment of inception."[22]

The Hopi also can approach the event from the perspective of the objective universe as well. In this case, the inceptive tense is used, which "refers to this edge of emergent manifestation...as the edge at which objectivity is attained; this is used to indicate beginning or starting. Whitehead might easily have employed the expective when discussing the emergence of eternal objects and the acting out of subjective aim, while using the inceptive to describe the processes of prehension and concrescence as actually experienced by actual occasions. Both of these tenses are related to each other in terms of process as well, since, as Whorf points out, "the inceptive, referring to the objective and result side implies the ending of the work of causation in the same breath that it states the beginning of manifestation."[23]

One cannot help but wonder how process thought might have developed had Whitehead had access to linguistic tools that encouraged his train of thought instead of impeding it, which English most certainly does. We can rejoice that our parts-mentality orientation is becoming obsolete, and that the world-views of Native peoples are finally being given the credence they deserve. It is truly ironic that for Whitehead (and for students of him) what seems like such a great—and difficult—conceptual leap is second nature and unquestioned reality for native populations all over the globe, most of whom have never even seen a copy of Whitehead's *Process and Reality*. But what treasures might await the fields of philosophy and science if somehow the marriage of the native mind and the scientific method could be achieved? What leaps might Process thought or systems theory be capable of in the hands of a Hopi philosopher or scientist with the proper tools for such exploration at hand? "What might the Native Mind glimpse that the scientist's more myopic gaze cannot?" Suzuki and Knudtson ask, "What creative images of the cosmos might holistic minds that are equally gifted intellectually conjure up if they were granted limitless access not just to the mind's reason but also to its capacity for feeling, compassion, visceral experience, and soaring imagination as it struggles to convey its personal vision of nature's boundlessness?"[24]

What, indeed.

NOTES

1   Suzuki, David and Peter Knudtson. *Wisdom of the Elders* (New York: Bantam Books, 1992), p. 17.

2   *Ibid.*, p. 30.

3   *Ibid.*, p. 31-2.

4   *Ibid.*, p. 3.

5   Fox, Matthew, OP, ed. *Meditations with Meister Eckhart* (Santa Fe: Bear & Co., 1982), p. 22.

6   Russell, Bertrand. *A History of Western Philosophy* (New York: Simon & Schuster, 1945), p. 733.

7   Hegel, quoted in Copleston, Frederick, SJ. *A History of Philosophy, Vol. VII* (New York: Doubleday, 1965), p. 170.

8   Mellert, quoting Whitehead, p. 58.

9   Suzuki, p. 16.

10 Alford, Dan Moonhawk. "God is Not a Noun in Native America" collected in *Foundations of Integral Linguistics Reader* (San Francisco, 1993), p. 2, 7.

11 *Ibid.*, p. 5.

12 Whorf, Benjamin Lee. *Language, Thought and Reality* (Massachusetts Institute of Technology, 1956), p. 59.

13 Mellert, Robert B. *What is Process Theology?* (New York: Paulist Press, 1975), p. 22.

14 Whorf, p. 59.

15 *Ibid.*, p. 60.

16 *Ibid.*

17 Whitehead, Alfred North, from Sherburne, Donald W., ed. *A Key to Whitehead's Process and Reality* (Chicago: The Free Press, 1966), p. 25.

18 *Ibid.*, p. 27.

19 Sahakian, William S. *History of Philosophy* (New York: Harper & Row, 1968), p. 297.

20 Mellert, p. 27.

21 Whitehead/Sherburne, p. 34.

22 Whorf, p. 60-61.

23 *Ibid.*, p. 61.

24 Suzuki, p. 14.

• PART FIVE •

Critical Views of Religion

Fundamentalism

Making Peace with the Prophets of Doom

There are few American subcultures as fanatical or dangerous as Protestant fundamentalism. In a society where pluralism must be fostered and understanding pursued, the
fundamentalists are public enemy number one. Great care must
be spent in our dealings; real compassion, too, if we are to make
any change.

Protestant fundamentalism is a highly legalistic religion that is
convinced that it isn't (Denial #1). All things, especially the
potentially ecstatic, are suspect: alcohol, dancing, swimming
(mixed) and touching the opposite sex before marriage; plus any
number of the pettiest of "sins": women wearing trousers, hair on
men touching their ears, etc. Fundamentalists have as their
authority "sola scriptura," elevating the King James (the
Authorized 1611) Version as the very breath of God. No authority is higher, not even the early Greek manuscripts. The Bible has
become, for them, a truly tyrannical "Paper Pope."
Fundamentalists preach a variant of Luther's doctrine of the
priesthood of the believer, while snatching the rug out from
beneath anyone who dares to interpret scripture differently than
they (Denial #2). Most fundamentalist positions have at their root

prejudice, fear, and ignorance, yet they claim a religious superiority for having all the answers (Denial #3).

"Having all the answers" is their primary draw. In a world as complex as ours has become, fundamentalists have retreated into "The Old-Time Gospel Hour" of early twentieth-century revivalism. Thinking is hard work, and avoided in our culture at all cost. This is the fundamentalists' ace in the hole. Their world is one of artificially determined stark blacks and whites, all the troublesome gray areas have been dealt with and there is no reason—indeed it would be sin—to question "Biblical authority."

The self-discipline required by living in a close community is also a draw. In most such churches, your business is everybody's business. "The walls have ears," and if you trip up you can be sure someone will be there to notice and begin the rumor mill. Being accountable to everyone is seen as an incentive, then.

For the sensitive person, fundamentalism is little more than slow suicide. Its foundation is in Calvinic dualism: one is ultimately not in control of one's eternal destiny (Predestination), so, one lives in fear, adhering strictly to the letter of the Law, suppressing all personality aspects that run counter to this law and at the same time hiding one's doubts and shortcomings from those one should trust most (members of one's community). This chronic suppression of the shadow is partly responsible for the massive projections fundamentalists cast on anyone not subscribing to their peculiar doctrines.

The affects on society are no better. In order to survive, a pluralistic society needs to be comfortable being just that. That means that the society appreciates and celebrates its diversity (i.e., maybe the Chinese couple across the hall crack you up with their cultural eccentricities, but you find them endearing and wouldn't have it any other way). As contemporary songwriter and prophet Bruce Cockburn says, "The whole of history is a growing together, if you want 'pure' you're gonna have caves again." There is a cultural tension, but that tension is what is cherished.

This is the fundamentalist's worst nightmare. The only right way is their way; to them difference = sin. The social tension mentioned above is perceived by them as a looming evil, threatening to the "people of God." Fundamentalists, even in casual conversation, will erect an "us vs. them" stance and relate to all things and everyone from this position. This offensive posturing makes dialogue difficult. If one tries to reason with them, one has become the silver-tongued serpent whispering lies to Eve. If the fundamentalist dream were to come true, America would become a fascist theocracy comparable to Orwell's *1984*. Witch hunts would become media events and racial hatred would set humanity back hundreds of years.

Ushering in a truly diverse society is going to require cooperation from everyone; how can America's fundamentalists be reached, befriended? It is not going to be easy, and strategy is not an inappropriate topic of discussion.

First of all, there are several theological roadblocks. Cooperation with other Christian churches, let alone non-Christian people of faith, is simply not something they pursue. They are "the elect" and everyone else is simply going to Hell. Major barriers are these:

- The authority of scripture/inerrancy
- Method of salvation (pray this prayer—zap! you're saved)
- Depraved nature of humankind
- Strict adherence to moral law as evidence of salvation
- Fulfillment of end-times prophesy

The gifts that Creation Spirituality have to give to the fundamentalist are, truly, the whole of the Gospel: liberation. Liberation from "sin-centricity"; liberation from the tyranny of the Law; a recognition that salvation is an on-going process that no one ever completes nor is ever without; that the Blessing is more important than the Curse; and the fulfillment of life, conscious of the Kingdom of God right here and now in us.

The barriers to Creation Spirituality are formidable, however. The fundamentalist lives with a built-in apocalypse detector, tuned in to anything that might be possible to interpret as a fulfillment of end-times prophesy, and unfortunately, Creation Spirituality sets it off like nothing we've ever seen before. First of all, Creation Spirituality comes from a Catholic source, and the Catholic church is (in fundamentalist eyes) the great Whore of

Babylon who fornicates with the Beast. Second, the idea of people of various religions worshipping together is the initial stages of the One World Religion that the Beast will officiate over. Couple these with the other alleged apocalyptic fulfillments in the culture at large—*perestroika*, the World Bank, the European Common Market, etc.—and the fundamentalist is sure to work him or herself up into a full-scale panic and will definitely not want to talk to us.

So what are we to do? How shall we proceed in our role as peacemakers? Biblical exegesis is out—the fundamentalist is in his or her home court there and will squarely squash us. Logic will not work, as the fundamentalist will always revert to Biblical authority and we end up once more with exegesis.

The only way to proceed is to retreat. If the fundamentalists won't talk, we won't talk. We won't fight either. We won't hate (that's a tough one). What will we do?

Just this: minister the Gospel; tell the Jesus story with our own lives, healing the sick, comforting the sorrowful, feeding the hungry, giving drink to the thirsty, clothing the naked and practising the difficult art of loving. Then they will have nothing to argue against. Oh, the fundamentalists will make Galatians 1:8 noises ("But though we, or an angel from heaven, preach any other gospel unto you than that which we have preached unto you, let him be accursed") but this will not hold up if it is clear that what we do, the Gospel we preach, is identical to the ministry of Jesus. Few Protestants, moderates or fundamentalists, dare say condemning words about Mother Theresa's work. How can they? She confounds them. ("How can she be a Catholic?") There are no barriers that can withstand dignity and love, not the paranoia of the deep South in the sixties, not the hardhearted British aristocracy in colonial India, and not the blind faith of American fundamentalists. As Paul says in Romans 12:20, "If thine enemy hunger, feed him; if he thirst give him drink: for in so doing thou shalt heap coals of fire on his head."

Finally, assuming some kind of fellowship can be established, what gifts does the fundamentalist tradition offer to us? For one thing, determination and resolution in ministry, and devotion to scripture. Their exegetical skills are unrivaled and their tradition of worship—sermon as sacrament—is dynamic, rich, and well-developed. There is great good in reconciliation, even with the most dangerous.

Our duty now, as Creation-centered theologians, is to be sensitive to our own prejudices, to eliminate them and learn to love such people as valiant persons of faith who bear enormous suffering. We can pray for them and visualize a change of heart. And most especially we can minister the Gospel, to them and to everyone. A study of the Gospels is all we need to see how we are to proceed. As Therese of Lisieux said, "Christ has no hands on earth but ours," so let us offer them, wounded and open.

That Naughty Bishop of Hippo

Dysfunctional Theological Innovations of St. Augustine

Even after fifteen hundred years, the mention of St. Augustine elicits strong reactions from people. From most, admiration, but there is a growing consensus that much of what is wrong in Western culture can be traced back to the severe neurosis of this most singular of the pre-medieval philosophers. A brilliant syncretist, Augustine succeeded Origen as the prime interpreter of neo-Platonic rhetoric in the Christian context, making creative Hellenistic leaps that rivaled even those of St. Paul. Brilliant though the leaps may be, they also considerably skewed the Christian vision. Orthodox scholar Fr. Michael Azkoul lists some of the good bishop's theological innovations that he (and a good many others) condemn: "...predestination and irresistible grace and...original sin; ...also his theory of Ideas and suspicious doctrine of creation; his crypto-Nestorian christology; his false mystagogy and understanding of Old Testament theophanies; his unorthodox ecclesiology; his philosophical conceptions of the soul; ...his speculations on purgatory, the beatific vision, his questionable view of deification; his anthropology and peculiar teaching on sex."[1] This is by no means an exhaustive list, and many of the items listed by Fr. Azkoul are beyond the scope of this paper. What we intend to consider are those doctrines which have had the most profound and destructive effects on Western culture, i.e. neo-Platonism and its attendant duality, free will, sexuality and women, original sin, and theocratic politics.

Neo-Platonism

Raised by a pagan father and a Christian mother, Augustine found the doctrine of the Manichaeans very attractive, as it seemed more logical and sophisticated than the Christianity of his childhood. But soon he found the teachings of Mani to be wanting, and discovered the writings of Plato and Plotinus. "Let Thales depart with his water," Augustine writes, "Anaximenes with the air, the Stoics with their fire, Epicurus with his atoms."[2] Plato, for him, was the tops. Neo-Platonism freed him from his materialism, and convinced him of the reality of an unseen world. Thus, having been moved by the sermons of St. Ambrose, he turned to the writings of St. Paul and began to view Christianity in a new light. Frederick Copleston, S.J. writes, "If neo-Platonism suggested to him the idea of the contemplation of spiritual things, of wisdom in the intellectual sense, the New Testament showed him that it was also necessary to lead a life in accordance with wisdom."[3] According to Bertrand Russell, Augustine was impressed that "Plato saw that God is not any bodily thing, but that all things have their being from God, and from something immutable.... He found in the Platonists the metaphysical doctrine of the Logos, but not the doctrine of the Incarnation and the consequent doctrine of human salvation."[4]

He also adapted the neo-Platonist concept of a hierarchical universe to the Christian mythos. "All natures are placed on three levels: God is at the top; the human soul stands in the middle; all bodies are on the lowest level. God is wholly immutable."[5] Knowledge, also, is organized on a hierarchical model. The lowest level of knowledge, sensation, is common to humanity and the beasts. The highest, the sole property of humankind, is the contemplation of the Ideals, or Wisdom. In between there is what Copleston calls a "kind of half-way house," where corporeal reality is compared and identified with the incorporeal.[6]

In Augustine's universe the world of forms took the shape of the mind of God, in which God is able to contemplate all of his finite potential in an infinite way. As Augustine describes it, "Creatures tend indeed to not-being, but as long as they are, they possess some form, and this is a reflection of the Form which can neither decline nor pass away. Thus the order and unity of Nature proclaims the unity of the Creator, just as the goodness of creatures, their positive reality, reveals the goodness of God and the order and stability of the universe manifest the wisdom of God. On the other hand, God, as 'the self-existent, eternal and immutable Being, is infinite, and, as infinite, incomprehensible'."[7]

Time and Predestination

The divine ideas themselves Augustine describes as "certain archetypal forms or stable and unchangeable reasons of things, which were not themselves formed but are contained in the divine mind eternally and are always the same. They neither arise nor pass away, but whatever arises and passes away is formed according to them."[8]

Time itself, then, in Augustine's universe is part of the material order and was nonexistent prior to the Creation. God resides in what Alan Watts has called "the Eternal Now," having neither beginning nor end, to whom time is present all at once. Bertrand Russell, though disagreeing with Augustine, considers this innovation to be "a great advance on anything to be found on the subject in Greek philosophy."[9] Says the Saint himself, "God is Himself in no interval nor extension of place, but in His immutable and pre-eminent might is both interior to everything because all things are in Him and exterior to everything because He is above all things. So too He is in no interval nor extension of time, but in His immutable eternity is older than all things because He is before all things and younger than all things because the same He is after all things."[10]

This sounds like wonderful, mystical, even panentheistic theology, but as M.D. Chenu makes clear, to Augustine, time "is a wound through which our life pours out. Decrepitude is the inevitable concomitant of man's existence. Man does not really exist except by and in the immutable eternity which awaits him.

In this obscure drama the world is not his home, and his history is only a temporary scaffolding."[11] As Azkoul describes it, he began to teach that "whatever happened in time happened with an unalterable purpose. One thing proceeds from another as a necessary conclusion from its premise. In retrospect, one can see that the past is what it is by necessity, with no options; likewise, the present rises from it and the future from the circumstances of the present."[12]

Not everyone is happy about Augustine's syncretism, to understate the matter. Among the Orthodox, it was stated in an eleventh century synod that "Anathema [are] those who devote themselves to Greek studies and instead of merely employing them as a part of their education, adopt the foolish doctrines of the ancients and accept them as truth. Anathema to those who firmly believe such doctrines and recommend them to others, whether secretly or overtly."[13]

Fr. Azkoul believes that Augustine's need to reconcile Platonism and Christianity—or in other words, "faith" and "reason"—was rooted in a deep-seated insecurity and served to comfort him regarding his salvation. "Augustine," he writes, "had indeed adopted 'the foolish doctrines of the ancients and accepted them as truth.' Hellenism was part of his thinking to the very end of his life."[14] The result of Augustine's doctrine of time was a grim form of predestination that was to root itself permanently in the Western psyche and surfaced in full force a thousand years later in the work of John Calvin.

Free Will

This line of thinking led Augustine to reinterpret the Genesis myth of Creation. As Elaine Pagels points out, what the Jews and early Christians had read for centuries as "a story of human freedom became, in his hands, a story of human bondage."[15] Instead of being a story about the gift of moral freedom, as St. John Chrysostom proclaimed, Augustine taught that "Adam's sin not only caused our mortality but cost us our moral freedom, irreversibly corrupted our experience of sexuality...and made us incapable of genuine political freedom."[16] Augustine then reinterpret-

ed the Pauline epistles through the lens of his theological innovations. Pagels calls the former interpretation of the myth "the heart
of the Christian gospel,"[17] and believes the "proclamation of
autexousia—the moral freedom to rule oneself" to be "virtually
synonymous with 'the gospel.'"[18]

In Augustine's version, which quickly became the accepted
position of the church, Adam and Eve were created with free will,
the choice between good and evil. They chose evil when they disobeyed God's command not to eat of the Tree of the Knowledge
of Good and Evil, and in that very moment, they were corrupted
through and through, to their very souls. The result of this is that
neither they nor their heirs were ever able to choose good again
of their own volition. Holiness, therefore, could only be had by a
gift of Divine Grace. The gift of grace, however, is given to only a
few, and with no observable system of selection. Salvation, to
Augustine, was a dice game, and as Russell points out, "St.
Augustine enumerates the sins committed by infants at the breast,
and does not shrink from the conclusion that infants who died
unbaptized go to Hell. The elect go to Heaven because God
chooses to make them the objects of His mercy: they are virtuous
because they are elect, not elect because they are virtuous."[19]
Therefore, Augustine insists that all of the church's members may
enjoy the Mysteries of the Sacraments, but only a few actually
receive their benefit. As Askoul writes, "Election is absolutely gra-
tuitous, indifferent to foreseen merits, preceding any good action
and wholly subordinated to God's arbitrary will. With no respect
to context, he extracted passages from Romans and other epistles
in order to prove his contention."[20]

Previous to this, Paul was perceived as meaning that the will's
incapacity to act autonomously was applicable only to the unbaptized. But Augustine, try as he might, could not reconcile this.
Azkoul asks, "How is God good, how merciful and just, if His
decision to save or reprobate is based on His secret Council wholly insensitive to human choices?"[21]

The effects of the fall were not limited to humanity, but were
cosmic in scale. According to Pagels, "Augustine insists that
through an act of will Adam and Eve [changed] the structure of

the universe; that their single, willful act permanently corrupted human nature as well as nature in general. Once harmonious, perfect, and free, now, through Adam's choice [human nature] is ravaged by mortality and desire, while all suffering, from crop failure, miscarriage, fever, and insanity to paralysis and cancer, is evidence of the moral and spiritual deterioration that Eve and Adam introduced...."[22]

Augustine was not without his contemporary critics, however. A Welshman named Palegius challenged his view, believing that free will was still operative for the human race, and that a person was able to live so as to be worthy of heaven. Unfortunately for Palegius, theological pluralism was not a fifth-century standard, and he was excommunicated for his common sense. Augustine insisted that his theology did not contradict free will. He claims that even in Christ a person is not delivered from Adam's curse. He might be relieved of Original Sin, but not its consequence, guilt—a burden inherited by infants upon their entry into the world regardless of their baptism.[23]

Sexuality

The immediately noticeable effect of the fall, for our first parents, was that their bodies no longer took orders from their brains. As Augustine puts it, "After Adam and Eve disobeyed...they felt for the first time a movement of disobedience in their flesh, as punishment in kind for their own disobedience to God.... The soul, which had taken a perverse delight in its own liberty and disdained to serve God, was now deprived of its original mastery over the body."[24] This doctrine came about as a result of Augustine's own personal sexual incontinence. Since lust was wont to violently overtake the saint, and since his "members" marched to their own drum, Augustine felt himself to be a victim, a captive, a slave to sin. Augustine uses inductive reasoning to make his case to the world. What he calls "this diabolical excitement of the genitals" must be common to all men (women we will examine later). Were it not for the "easy out" of marriage, "people would have intercourse indiscriminately, like dogs."[25] (A hilarious side note is that, in his wild youth, he knew that what he was doing was wrong, and would pray that God would "give me chastity, but not yet."[26])

This teaching was in direct contradiction to the Apostolic Fathers. Clement of Alexandria, in fact, criticized celibates "who say that they are 'imitating the Lord,' who never married, nor had any possessions in the world, and who boast that they understand the gospel better than anyone else."[27]

Many of Augustine's contemporaries disagreed with his interpretations, as well. One such dissenter, Jovinian, objected and attempted to prove by biblical authority that celibates were no holier than married folk. Augustine replied that "the fecundity of a married woman was not comparable in value to the fecundity of the virgin, who produced souls for Christ," and many others supported this view.[28] Once again, disagreeing with the Bishop of Hippo was proved a dangerous undertaking, and eventually Jovinian too was excommunicated.

According to feminist theologian Rosemary Radford Reuther, Augustine considered the blessings given to marriage (as recorded in scripture) to apply only under the dispensation of the Old Covenant, that of God with the Jews.[29] This view was supported by Clement, who believed that legitimate procreation is a blessing applicable throughout time,[30] although he would probably have conceded that recreational sex, even for married folk, was sin.

Women

Augustine's dim view of sex extended its corruption to women. He writes, "I feel that nothing so casts down the manly mind from its heavenly heights as the fondling of woman and those bodily contacts which belong to the married state."[31] Good Christians are exhorted by him to simultaneously love a woman's personality, yet "to hate in her the corruptible and mortal conjugal connection, sexual intercourse, and all that pertains to her as a wife."[32] Women do not even bear the image of God, according to Augustine, unless they are joined to a man.[33]

Women are therefore subordinate in all ways to men. This was the standard view, but few took it to Augustine's inhuman extremes. Pagels points out that in Julian's view, "Man's rule over woman forms part of the order of nature, 'an institution of nature, not a punishment for sin.'"[34] Augustine even teaches that a woman has no personal rights over her own body, but "must surrender her body to her husband on command, receiving from such use no personal pleasure, but allowing herself to be used solely as an instrument of procreation."[35] "Even in paradise," Reuther writes, "the male would have 'used' the woman without sensual feeling, just as he moves his hand or foot, dispassionately, and totally under control of the rational will. There would have been no uncontrolled rush of disordered affection and spontaneous tumescence of the male sexual organ. But the male would have sowed his seed in the woman with the same objectivity as a farmer sows seed in field."[36] Reuther elsewhere notes that Augustine's views on sex won him new accusations of promoting Manichaen teachings, which he refuted, claiming that the abominable means ultimately achieve a good end in the blessing of birth. (Ironically, the good bishop also maintained that prostitutes are necessities, much like a sewer in a palace. If you take away the sewer, the palace becomes filthy![37])

Original Sin

The result of Augustine's take on Eden was his concept of Original Sin. Though he claims biblical authority, many scholars, now and then, believe him to be solely responsible for its manufacture. Sexual desire, for him was proof of, and according to Pagels, punishment for, universal Original Sin.[38] Augustine reasoned that Original Sin must be hereditary, otherwise there was no explanation for why babies had to endure suffering. To deny this was to deny that there was justice in the universe. "You must explain," he writes, "why such great innocence is sometimes born blind or deaf. If nothing deserving punishment passes from parents to infants, who could bear to see the image of God sometimes born retarded, since this afflicts the soul itself? Consider the plain facts; consider why some infants suffer from a demon."[39] Thus, in a world where there are no easy answers, Augustine felt justified to invent his own. Augustine, in fact, believed babies to be so infected that until they were baptized he conceived of them as the very limbs of Satan![40]

"If infants are not sinners," Augustine asked Palegius, "Why then are they baptized?" Palegius' poetic response was that the intention of baptism was for "...spiritual illumination, adoption to divine sonship, citizenship in the heavenly Jerusalem, admission to the fellowship of Christ, and possession of the Kingdom of God"—an ennobling response, and very like what a modern catechism might say.[41]

Ironically, though it is the woman who is corruption personified, it is through the male issue that the Original Sin is actually transmitted: it is the semen which is the bearer of death. In creating a new creature, it is the woman who provides the body, from her substance, and the man who gives the soul, which is already corrupt. This theory is called Traducianism.[42] Fr. Azkoul points out, however, that "Augustine was unhappy with Traducianism, because it implied a material conception of the soul, a conception wholly uncongenial to his Platonism, which...presents the soul as completely spiritual."[43] He feared, however, that if the theory were discounted there would be no justification for infant baptism (excepting Palegius' reasoning), for "if God injected the created soul directly into the body, then, the guilt of Adam's sin could not pass from parent to child."[44]

As in his own time, many if not most clerical opinions in the majority of traditions now reject Augustine's explanation. "We do not inherit the 'guilt' of Adam," Azkoul firmly states. "Human beings are victims of Adam's sin, not the bearers of it. We inherit not his sin, but the propensity to sin." Fr. Matthew Fox asks us "What trust is lost in oneself, in one's body, in the cosmos, when children are instructed that they came into the world as blotches on God's creation?"[45]

Augustine's proof text proves to be even more of an embarrassment. He uses Romans 5:12, "Wherefore, as by one man sin entered into the world, and death by sin; and so death passed upon all men, for that all have sinned" (KJV). Saying that, Paul claims that death is visited upon humanity because of Adam, "in whom all sinned." In the Greek, this prepositional phrase reads εφ ω, which is properly translated "in as much as," or "because" not "in whom."[46]

Augustine is clearly out of line with the prior teachings of the Church, and is refuted by Christians of his own time and ours alike. Elaine Pagels notes that his theory contradicts two key beliefs of the Christian faith: the goodness of God's creation and the freedom of the human will. Even those who accept the idea of inherited sin believe that baptism eradicates this defect completely, so that we can say with Didymus the Blind "now we are found once more such as we were when we were first made: sinless and masters of ourselves."[47]

Duality

Although Augustine professed to have denounced his former beliefs in the doctrines of Mani and wrote copious refutations of his heresies, the profound dualism espoused by his former teacher did not depart him. This became troublesome for Augustine, not only in the theory of Traducianism noted above, but in his conception of the Incarnation itself. Augustine could not conceive that the Spirit of Christ could actually join itself to the corrupt nature of the flesh. As he says, "For as the soul makes use of the body in a single person to form a man, so God makes use of a man in a single person to form Christ. In the former person, there is a mingling of soul and body; in the latter, a mingling of God and man...when the Word of God unites to the soul which has a body, taking thereby both soul and body at once.... It ought to be easier to intermingle two incorporeal things rather than one incorporeal and the other corporeal."[48] So, in Augustine's view, the soul was the middle man which enabled Jesus to be united in body and Spirit without the one having to be joined to the other (which is positively Gnostic!).

Most of us today would agree with Chenu that "it is not only the soul that thinks, nor only the body that senses; it is the man [sic] who thinks, wills, loves, senses, acts, works. Body and soul are not real subjects each of which has in itself the capacity to be or to act in its own sphere, merely conditioned by the other."[49] But this holistic view of humankind was unthinkable for

Augustine. Matthew Fox believes that if there is such a thing as Original Sin, that sin is not Adam's disobedience in the garden, but is in fact dualism itself. For, according to him, it is dualism which "divides and thereby conquers, pitting one's thoughts against one's feelings, one's body against one's spirit, one's political vocation against one's personal needs, people against earth, animals, and nature in general."[50] Representing the Creation tradition, Julian gives us the elements of an integrated Christian faith in what he calls the five praises: "the praise of Creation; the praise of marriage; the praise of the law; the praise of the saints; the praise of the will."[51]

Communal vs. Individual Sin

It was during the intertestamental period that a significant shift in Jewish theology began to rear its head, one which would be seized by Augustine and used to promote a dysfunctionally introverted spirituality: the displacement of the emphasis on communal sin in favor of an individual variety. In classical Jewish theology, Israel sinned and was restored to favor as a people, not primarily as individuals. But since the Church could not sin, the doctrine of a new "individualized" salvation was adopted by Augustine. Bertrand Russell notes that sin is connected with self-importance.[52] This smacks of a perverse, inverted narcissism, which Stendahl says Augustine "turned in on himself, infatuated and absorbed by the question not of when God will send deliverance in the history of salvation, but how God is working in the innermost individual soul."[53] The church had always proclaimed herself to be the refuge of all, not merely of the few. But, as addressed above in the section on free will, Augustine followed the lead of his teachers Plato, Plotinus, and Mani in proclaiming an elitist salvation reserved for "the elect" whom God chooses independent of human vice or virtue, apparently arbitrarily.

And it is in this primary shift of focus that Augustine misses completely the cosmological ramifications of the gospel. "Too much guilt," writes Fox, "too much introspection, too much preoccupation with law, sin, and grace rendered Augustine, and the theology that was to prevail in his name for sixteen centuries in the West, oblivious of what the Eastern Christian church cele-brates as *theosis*, the divinization of the cosmos."[54] Leo Scheffczyk, in his study *Creation and Providence,* charges that "the harmony which St. Augustine established at the level of ontolog-ical thought was achieved at the expense of the scriptural concept of Creation as part of the economy of salvation."[55] Augustine would have us not look beyond ourselves for our experience of God, but only inward. He simply ignores the cosmological rami-fications of the Fall and redemption in favor of a model which would support his neo-platonist cosmology. Julian responds to this view by saying that calling the Earth "'cursed in [Adam's] works' expresses the viewpoint of a person who is spiritually dying...this lie cannot injure nature, nor the earth, in this curse, but only his own person, and his own will."[56] Azkoul notes that only Platonists seem to see creation as a "problem."[57]

Politics

It might be that Augustine's ideas would not have met such widespread acceptance had it not been for the changing political climate. Before the emperor Constantine's conversion, the gospel's message of radical freedom provided profound meaning for those Christians who felt persecuted by pagan society and traditions. Christianity gave to people a cosmic context compared to which the material realities of Roman life seemed insignificant and imprisoning. But once the empire embraced the Christian faith, suddenly the radical freedom was no longer so radical, and the truly devout had to search out other lifestyles which would fill this hole in their faith life. Many went to the desert to live out their days before God in silent reverence. But this was not the way for everybody, and thus it is that Augustine's theories made sense out of the new political situation. Elaine Pagels explains it thus: "What Augustine says, in simplest terms, is this: human beings cannot be trusted to govern themselves, because our very nature—indeed, all of nature—has become corrupt as the result of Adam's sin. In the late fourth and the fifth century...Augustine's theory of human depravity—and correspondingly, the political means to control it—replaced the previous ideology of human freedom."[58]

Thus, when Rome was under Pagan rule, it was maintained by evil means, such as injustice and violence, but now that it is Christian, it will be a truly just and moral state, which will produce moral men and women.[59] In the prior arrangement, the state religion was under control of the state. But under Christianity, the state was under control of the Church.[60]

The shift in power, not surprisingly, was attended by a shift in behavior on the part of the Church. When the Donatists complained of the Church using imperial forces to enforce the will of its hierarchy, Augustine increasingly turned to force through everything from the denial of civil rights, fines, penalties, to exile and physical coercion. As Pagels writes, "By insisting that humanity, ravaged by sin, now lies helplessly in need of outside intervention, Augustine's theory could not only validate secular power but justify as well the imposition of church authority—by force if necessary—as essential for human salvation."[61]

Conclusion

Although it is obvious that Augustine occasionally contradicted himself, especially in the comparison of his early with his later works, as Fr. Azkoul says, each of his doctrinal errors "is consistent with all his others, stemming from principles which allowed him to elaborate a peculiar and coherent body of religious opinion. His theology, cosmology, christology, mystagogy, historiosophy, etc., are interwoven."[62] Augustine searched the scriptures relentlessly to find support for his theories, which in his imagination had become the Catholic Tradition. Reuter notes that in searching for support for predestination, Augustine did not adopt the theory after patient and careful study, but in "the fury of the dialectical hunt."[63] Reuter goes on to observe that Augustine so changed the face of Western Christendom that he prepared it for division with the East.[64] Azkoul's book *The Influence of Augustine of Hippo on the Orthodox Church*, so often quoted here, is a monumental refutation of Augustine's heresies that the Orthodox tradition could not, and cannot, embrace. Azkoul quotes one Orthodox saint as saying "We can only thank God that the doctrine of the Eastern Church was formulated outside the sphere of Augustinianism, which we must consider as alien to us.[65]

The political, global, and psychological dilemmas of our time are not those of Augustine's, and his formulations are no longer applicable in our society. Even in his own time there were those who believed him to be in grave error. His rival Julian believed his inventions to be "false, many foolish, and many are sacrilegious."[66] Augustine was fond of saying that his Platonist God "is never disturbed by any passions." Matthew Fox believes that this tells us a lot more about Augustine than about God.[67]

NOTES

1 Azkoul, Michael. *The Influence of Augustine of Hippo on the Orthodox Church* (Lewiston: Edwin Mellen Press, 1990), p. 7.

2 Russell, Bertrand, quoting Augustine. *A History of Western Philosophy* (New York: Simon and Schuster, 1945), p. 358.

3 Copleston, Frederick, S.J. *A History of Philosophy, Volume II* (New York: Image, 1962), pp. 42-43.

4 Russell, pp. 351, 358.

5 Bourke, Vernon, ed. *The Essential Augustine* (Indianapolis: Hackett Publishing Co., 1964), p.43.

6 Copleston, p. 57.

7 Copleston, quoting Augustine, p. 72.

8 *Ibid.*, p. 73.

9 Russell, p. 354.

10 Copleston, quoting Augustine, p. 72.

11 Chenu, M.D. *Faith and Theology* (New York: MacMillan, 1968), p. 126.

12 Azkoul, p. 185.

13 *Ibid.*, p. 139.

14 *Ibid.*, p. 139.

15 Pagels, Elaine. *Adam, Eve, and the Serpent* (New York: Random House, 1988) p. xxvi.

16 *Ibid.*, p. xxvi.

17 *Ibid.*, p. 126.

18 *Ibid.*, p. 99.

19 Russell, Bertrand; Al Seckel, ed. *On God and Religion* (Buffalo: Prometheus, 1986), p. 274.

20 Azkoul, p. 190.

21 *Ibid.*, p. 207.

22 Pagels, p. 133-4.

23 Azkoul, p. 203.

24 Pagels, quoting Augustine, p. 110.

25 *Ibid.*, p. 140.

26 Russell, *History...*, p. 348.

27 Pagels, p. 21.

28 McLaughlin, Eleanor Commo. "Equality of Souls, Inequality of Sexes: Woman in Medieval Theology," from *Religion and Sexism*, Rosemary Radford Reuther, ed. (New York: Touchstone, 1974), p. 231.

29 Reuther, Rosemary Radford. "Patristic Spirituality and the Experience of Women in the Early Church," from *Western Spirituality,* Matthew Fox, ed., p. 149.

30 Pagels, p. 27.

31 Reuther, p. 149.

32 Reuther, Rosemary Radford. "Virginal Feminism in the Fathers of the Church" from *Religion and Sexism*, Rosemary Radford Reuther, ed. (New York: Touchstone, 1974), p. 161.

33 Reuther, "Patristic Spirituality..." p. 148.

34 Pagels, 137.

35 Reuther, "Virginal..." p. 164.

36 Reuther, "Patristic..." p. 147.

37 O'Faolain, Julia and Lauro Marines, eds. *Not in God's Image* (New York: Harper, 1973), p. 291.

38 Pagels, p. xviii.

39 *Ibid.*, p. 135.

40 Russell, *History...*, p. 365.

41 Azkoul, p. 198

42 *Ibid.*, p. 184.

43 *Ibid.*, p. 184.

44 *Ibid.*, p. 184.

45 Fox, p. 58.

46 St. Paul, Romans 5:12 from *The Zondervan Parallel New Testament in Greek and English* (Grand Rapids: Zondervan, 1975), p. 455.

47 Pagels, p. 131.

48 Azkoul, quoting Augustine, p. 229.

49 Chenu, p. 49.

50 Fox, p. 54.

51 Pagels, p. 136.

52 Russell, *History...*, p. 346.

53 Fox, p. 209.

54 *Ibid.*, p. 76.

55 Scheffczyk, Leo. *Creation and Providence* (New York: Herder and Herder, 1970), p. 103.

56 Pagels, p. 138.

57 Azkoul, p. 247.

58 Pagels, p. 145.

59 Copleston, pps. 87, 89.

60 Russell, *History...*, p. 362.

61 Pagels, pps. 124-5.

62 Azkoul, p. 221.

63 *Ibid.*, p. 196.

64 *Ibid.*, p. 10.

65 *Ibid.*, p. 3.

66 Pagels, p. 136.

67 Fox, p. 63.

Second-Guessing God

With the turn of the millennium only a few years away, it is inevitable that millennarian panic will be heating up as it gets nearer. The beginnings are already visible: more street preachers than ever warn of the impending wrath of God, and the TV evangelists are already pumping the apocalypse for every dime it may yield. I am concerned, however, for the faith of those who take the Bible's poetic depictions of the second coming of Christ as literal truth, who will be convinced by their leaders that the year 2000 will be the Day of the Lord, when Jesus will return and those who are "true believers" will be caught up to meet him in the air. This will be followed by many years of abject horror for those who are left.

This doctrine of "meeting Christ in the air," known as "the Rapture," is taught by evangelical Christian denominations all over the world. It is based on a single verse from 1 Thessalonians, (4:16) the only one in scripture to allude to such an event, and its authorship (traditionally attributed to Paul) is universally questioned. Evangelicals set this as a central puzzle piece to an elaborate "plan" for the end times, picking and choosing throughout the biblical text for other pieces to complete their complex and unlikely scenario.

Many evangelicals are surprised to discover that the "Rapture" has no place in the historical doctrine of the church, and has only been in existence for less than two hundred years. Catholic scholarship has typically—and wisely—opted not to construct a dogmatic interpretation for the book of Revelation and other biblical material that is usually thought of as pertaining to the "end-times." What has happened, though, is that nearly every generation of disgruntled Christians has used these scriptures to justify their own shortsighted agendas. None of them have been correct.

At the turn of the first millennium, just this sort of speculation resulted in panic throughout all of Christendom. Richard Erdoes writes that "on the last day of the year 999...the old basilica of St. Peter's at Rome was thronged with a mass of weeping and trembling worshippers awaiting the end of the world.... Many of those present had given away all their possessions to the poor...in order to assure for themselves forgiveness...at the Last Judgment. Many poor sinners...had entered the church in sackcloth and ashes, having already spent weeks and months doing penance and mortifying the flesh.... Many signs appeared.... French nuns saw fiery armies fighting in the sky [and] in Aquitaine, the sky rained blood." Obviously, the Lord did not return, and much injustice and suffering was born as the result of this madness.

Those in every tradition who are fundamentalist regarding their belief inevitably run into trouble. In the last two centuries before the Common Era, the Jews anticipated the coming of the "Son of Man," a mythological figure found in the book of Daniel and in many non-biblical apocalypses popular at the time. The Son of Man, it was believed, was the anointed one of God who would come as a great warrior, descending from the clouds with the hosts of heaven, crushing the Roman Empire. He would then set up Jerusalem as his capitol and would rule the Earth for a thousand years.

According to the Christian tradition, it didn't happen that way at all. The messiah came quietly, born of a peasant woman. Instead of crushing the Romans, he was crushed by them, dying a criminal's death.

It seems to me we would do well to learn from the mistakes of the past. The Jewish fundamentalists of the time were so sure of their own interpretation of the apocalypse that the messiah passed unseen under their noses. The Evangelical myth of the apocalypse is frighteningly similar to that of the Jews of Jesus' day—what reason have we to think that they may be any more correct in their expectations?

It is my opinion that it is impossible to second-guess God. When Christ returns, I don't believe it will be according to any-one else's agenda, certainly not those being tossed about in the attempt to frighten people into the "fold." In my experience, this is not God's way.

The Jewish understanding of the coming of the messiah has undergone a meaningful evolution; in the Talmud, the coming of the messiah has come to be understood as a personal encounter of faith. It is my hope that our understanding could also progress beyond the literal. I think it less likely that Christ will return in bodily form than that he will come in a more ideological fashion. The second coming may be upon us when the human race final-ly realizes the divinity inherent in all of Creation, and recognizes the Cosmic Christ at the heart of all things. Perhaps the second coming will be as Teilhard de Chardin describes it, as the Omega point—the culmination of evolution—towards which we are drawn by the love of God. These are possibilities to which our minds and spirits should be open.

Above all, we need to remember Jesus' own injunction against those who say they "know" when his return will come, when he said "of that day and hour no one knows, not even the angels in heaven, not even the Son; only the Father." All of the world's great faith traditions look forward to a coming Reign of God, when jus-tice and peace will be known in all the Earth. Let us not be deceived by those who would sell us an apocalypse unworthy of a God of Love.

Apocalypse Now?

No, But Maybe by the Time You Read This...

Is the end of the world coming soon? It will be, if the most powerful lobby in America has its way. For the past twenty years, American politics has been rocked by an organizing effort no one saw coming, and no one—not even long-time, traditional Republicans—has been able to stop. They have been known by a multitude of names: the Moral Majority, Evangelical America, the Christian Right, among others.

They are empowered, they are in power, and they are doing everything *in* their power to bring about the end of the world. Not figuratively, not hyperbolically, not the end-of-the-world-as-we-know-it. They are meeting in their boardrooms, in their churches, and in the halls of Congress to plan, instigate, and bring about Armageddon. They are not doing it clandestinely, or euphemistically, there are no winks or nods accompanying their discussions. They are doing it out in the open, preaching about it in their churches, publishing about it in what amounts to literally forests worth of trees, and discussing strategies for it at White House luncheons.

They have put one of their own in the White House, and they have been steering the great ship of state in a beeline for worldwide holocaust. Imagine Jerry Falwell astride Slim Pickins' bomb in Kubrick's *Dr. Strangelove,* waving his Bible and hooting and hollering all the way to point zero, and you get the idea. We are headed towards global destruction, and Evangelical America couldn't be happier about it.

As Dr. Mike Evans of the Evangelical Israel Broadcasting Network once crowed, the War with Iraq is a "dress rehearsal for Armageddon"[1] and plenty of conservative Christians agreed with their whole-hearted support for the effort. Evangelicals have also backed the Israeli political hard-line, sabotaging any efforts toward a peaceful resolution, since a Jewish-controlled Israel is imperative to their end-time scenario. A showdown in the Middle East between Muslims and a united Christian-Jewish block is exactly what they are after, since in their end-times schema, such a conflagration *must* occur before Jesus can return.

Apocalypse-bent organizations such as the United Pentecostal Church's Apostolic Congress are so influential that the White House consults them on Middle East policy, and, as the record shows, acts in accord with their wishes. As Pentecostal minister Robert G. Upton boasted, "We're in constant contact with the White House. I'm briefed at least once a week via telephone...I was there about two weeks ago.... At that time we met with the president."[2]

Since, according to a recent Gallup Poll, 42% of Americans consider themselves "born again," this is by no means an insignificant voting block. The truly frightening fact is that the vast majority of born-again Christians buy into this apocalyptic mania. They desire with all their hearts to see the Prince of Peace returning on the clouds in glory, and they don't care what kind of violence they have to engineer to make it happen.

And strangely, the otherwise level-headed contingent of Americans—the old-guard Republicans, the liberals, even the radicals—seem to be yawning and looking the other way. There aren't even any Chicken Littles suggesting that the sky might be looking a bit heavier than usual. America is on a Lemmings' March, the cliff is getting closer, and no one seems to care.

How did such a bizarre scenario come about? How did we get to this, one of the most volatile cultural standoffs in history? It all started in the Middle East, and if the Christian Right has its way, it will end there as well.

Zarathustra and the Birth of Apocalypticism

It all began with a Vedic priest named Zarathustra almost three thousand years ago. Vedism is a primitive form of Hinduism brought to both India and the Middle East by marauding hordes of Aryans thousands of years ago. They conquered the native populations and imposed on them the Vedic gods, setting up social hierarchies with the clergy, conveniently, taking their place as the top dogs.

Of course, power always breeds corruption, and the Vedic priests were not immune to such universal human phenomena. The corruption of the Vedic priesthood led to three reform movements in India—Buddhism, Jainism, and Upanishadic Hinduism—but in Persia, there was only one: Zoroastrianism.

"Zoroaster" is a sloppy Greek transliteration of Zarathustra's name, but it stuck. Zarathustra actually means, "the golden light," or "that guy with the yellow camel"—the language of the early Zoroastrian scriptures is often obscure, so take your pick as to the meaning you like best. Zarathustra had a vision in which it was revealed to him that all the Vedic gods were not gods at all, but angels in a divine hierarchy with one God, Ahura Mazda ("the Wise God") ruling over all. According to Zarathustra, all the Vedic gods still had the same duties as before; they just suffered a demotion in status.

Second in command was Spenta Mainyu, the Holy Spirit, who executed Mazda's will in the world. Interestingly, Spenta had a twin of equal power who was in opposition to the divine hierarchy. Known as Angra Mainyu, the "Evil Spirit," this being headed up a "lowerarchy" of demonic beings hell-bent on destroying Mazda's good creation.

This is how Zarathustra understood the presence of evil and suffering in the world: this planet is a battlefield, and humans are caught in the cosmic crossfire. We must, inevitably, choose sides—for not to choose sides is to side with evil by default. Of course, Zarathustra exhorted his followers to choose Mazda and

THE APOCALYPSE IN THE WORLD'S RELIGIONS

Since this article focuses on Zoroastrian, ancient Jewish, and Christian eschatology ("study of final things"), let's look at how the rest of the world sees The End: **Hindu theology** teaches that Vishnu is sleeping and dreaming the world. From his navel sprouts Brahma, the Creator, and every time Brahma opens his eyes, the universe begins a cycle of being, lasting millions of years. Every time he closes his eyes the universe comes to an end. When he opens his eyes again, it all starts up again, in an endless cycle. Let's hope you are reading this with greater comprehension than the last time you sat there reading this—what, 115 million years ago? My how time flies.... **Buddhist theology** teaches that the world will eventually forget the Buddha's teaching, and when that happens, everything will just go to hell, until the Meitraya Buddha emerges from the Tusita Heaven to renew the Dharma on earth and to begin a new kalpa, or "world cycle".... **Islamic eschatology** has Jesus, not Muhammed, coming back at the end of time. According to Hadith (Traditions of the Prophet), he will descend to the earth, smash all the crosses and kill every pig (no more ham on Easter, Christians). Then Jesus will slay Iblis (Satan) with an actual sword, and will usher in an age of peace.

Fortunately, not all religious views of what constitutes a "happy ending" involve reducing the planet to a pile of ashes. Contemporary, **liberal Judaism** sees the coming of the messiah as a figurative one. When there is peace and justice in every land, when none go hungry or homeless, then the tikkun olam, the "repair of the world" will be complete and the messiah will truly be among us, more a Messianic Age than a real person. **Liberal Christians** see the second coming of Jesus in almost exactly the same terms, and liberal Buddhists understand the coming of Meitraya Buddha in the same way. Thus, unlike the fundamentalists of almost every stripe who are trying to coax history into a cosmic cardiac arrest, liberal believers of many different faith traditions are working side-by-side to build a world free of war, disease, and hunger. This kind of religious perspective could give us reason to hope, could allow us to dream of a better future, and inspire us to work towards it in the here-and-now—if only such a vision could catch on! Maybe a series of best-selling novels...hm....

to join in the battle for the fate of the world. Zarathustra wrote his revelations down in a collection of poetry called the *Gathas*, the primary scriptures of Zoroastrianism. The *Gathas* predicts the coming cataclysmic battle in which history will come to a head, evil will be ultimately defeated, and good will triumph at tremendous cost.

As you might expect, Zarathustra's fellow Vedic priests were less than enamored of this revelation, and they vowed to hunt him down and kill him. Zarathustra and his followers fled and finally ended up in the kingdom of Balkh, in present-day Afghanistan. The King of Balkh was swayed by the prophet's teaching and offered the fledgling religion a safe haven. From there, missionaries carried Zarathustra's revelation back into Persia until, a few generations later, it became the dominant religion of the Persian empire, entirely supplanting the Vedism that gave it birth.

The Jews Discover the Apocalypse

Zarathustra's apocalyptic revelations might have ended up as an odd footnote in religious history had the Persians kept to themselves. But no, they were an empire, and conquering neighboring peoples seems to invariably go with that territory. In the eighth century BCE the Persians conquered Judah, and carried the Jewish people into captivity in Babylon. While they were there, they underwent a profound change in their theology. The Zoroastrians introduced them to ideas such as angels, demons, heaven, hell, and, of course, the apocalypse.

The Jewish people ate it up, swallowing much of Zoroastrian theology whole, and running the rest of it through a thin Jewish filter. It is not hard to see why the apocalyptic message of the Persian prophet was so influential, either. While Zarathustra and his crew were on the run from homicidal Vedic priests, the cosmic battlefield metaphor gave them great comfort. Regardless of how much they were suffering now, Mazda was one day going to avenge them on their enemies and put all things right. This kind of revenge fantasy had a great deal of appeal, and the Jews appropriated it to their own ends.

Soon they began writing their own apocalyptic literature, such as the book of Daniel, patterned very closely on the Zoroastrian roadmap of the end-of-time. Only, in their version, it was the God of Israel who would avenge them on their Zoroastrian captors. The Jews even gave their own name to the arch-nemesis of the One God: Satan, Hebrew for the "adversary."

The Zoroastrian theology stuck, and even after the Jews were liberated and returned to Israel, they were soon to be conquered by other world powers, most notably, Rome. Suddenly, more Jewish apocalypses hit the best-sellers lists, only this time, it was Rome who would be the target of God's revenge at the rapidly-approaching end-of-time. They saw Rome as the agent of Satan in a cosmic battle for the fate of the earth, and they awaited the arrival of the messiah ("anointed one" or "king") who would appear on a white horse and lead God's armies against the infernal foe, liberating Israel from oppression and setting up Jerusalem as the capitol of the world—which would be benevolently governed, of course, by the Jews.

Christian Apocalypticism

When Jesus came on the scene, the Jewish people were in an apocalyptic frenzy. Apocalyptic thinking is always rampant when a people are oppressed, and Rome's stranglehold on Israel fanned the eschatological flames into a bonfire that threatened daily to upset the fragile peace of the area. The early Christians appropriated much of the Jewish religion into their own, including their fondness for the Apocalypse. When the persecution of the fledgling Christian church under Nero threatened to extinguish the movement, the book of Revelation recast Zarathustra's revenge fantasy, with Jesus in the role of Spenta Mainyu, and the Beast as Satan's representative in the great and coming battle.

The book of Revelation only made it into the Bible by the smallest of margins—many early church fathers argued against it, as they felt there were worthier—and less profoundly weird—books to consider. But the book had sufficient support to carry its inclusion, much to the bloody misfortune of countless victims of its misinterpretations throughout the church's history. For nearly

THE HISTORY OF THE RAPTURE

Protestant apocalypticism got a huge boost in the nineteenth century when a blind, teenage Scottish mystic named Margaret McDonald had a vision of the Rapture, the event in which Jesus appears in the sky, and all those who are "born again" shed their clothes and rise up into the sky to meet their Lord. The Rapture is entirely McDonald's invention—the doctrine had never been heard of in the history of Christianity until then. An English Separatist preacher named Darby picked up McDonald's vision and ran with it—all the way to America, where he influenced a man preparing a study Bible by the name of Scofield. Scofield incorporated McDonald's ideas into his own "dispensational" theology, and once his Bible became the standard text in American Evangelicalism, her ideas gradually became undisputed doctrine.

Rapture theology was a quiet, well kept secret of the Evangelical American subculture until the 1970s, when a little book called *The Late Great Planet Earth* by Hal Lindsey became a best seller. Suddenly cries of "Jesus is Coming!" were heard in every church in the nation, and ever since the Evangelical publishing machine has barely been able to keep up with the demand for End-Times material, fiction and "non-fiction" alike.

a thousand years it was largely ignored—seen as a prophesy that had already come to pass when Christianity effectively "conquered" the known world. But the Protestant reformation reignited interest in the book, casting the Pope as the new anti-Christ, whose bloody war on the protesters would surely be avenged by God any day now. Once again, the math is easy to do: persecution + religion = apocalypticism.[3]

Protestantism has always loved the book of Revelation, because once they freed themselves from the Catholics, there were always other Protestants to be oppressed by. Recasting the role of the Antichrist is a perennial entertainment that never ceases to amuse and delight Christians who feel under someone else's thumb.[4]

Which only begs the question: if apocalypticism is always born of oppression, what accounts for the apocalyptic boom in America in the past thirty years? In what way could Evangelicals—who in the past twenty years have risen to become the richest,[5] most successful, politically empowered block in American politics today—possibly construe themselves as an oppressed people?

Christianity Under Attack

It's the culture war. The "leftist elites" are, in the Evangelicals' estimation, doing everything they can to erode all that is holy in American life today. Hollywood and television are attacking morals, science is waging a bloody assault on Biblical creationism in every classroom in the nation, and those damned (literally) gays and lesbians are clawing away at the God-ordained and pristine institution of marriage. And to add insult to injury, the televangelists, with their televised sexual exploits, have made Evangelicals the laughingstock of the urbane Western world.

In their view, traditional values and the Christian religion have never been under such heavy assault. It is no wonder that every Evangelical who has ever read a *Left Behind* novel (and that's at least a good sixty million of them and counting, folks) is scanning the skies looking for Jesus to appear in the clouds, rapture them up to heaven, and unleash hell on earth to vindicate them against all their godless, secular, homo-lovin' enemies.[6]

It's no wonder that the Evangelicals are fighting back. It's no wonder they've got their war paint on, taking Congress and the White House, rolling back abortion and sex education programs, protecting the sacred institution of marriage, and, now that they've gotten a taste of power, doing everything they can to engineer the End of Days according to their peculiar interpretation of scripture. They want Jesus to return, they want to strike back at those evil secularists pushing their sexual immorality and frightening post-modern non-paradigms. They want the bad guys to suffer and good guys to win in the end, and the sooner the better. And they have no doubt about who the good guys are: them, and only them. Evanglical America. So praise God and pass the ammunition.

Armageddon is Coming—By Any Means Necessary

The rest of us godless heathen really ought to be asking ourselves some hard questions. Like this one: Is it really appropriate to allow the three-thousand-year-old revenge fantasy of a hallucinating Vedic priest to govern contemporary foreign policy? Because *it is*. And we can either do something to stop it or we can sit back and enjoy the fireworks. And the fireworks are coming—just look in the direction of the Middle East for the best view.

The image of the sad, lonely prophet carrying a sign saying "The End is Near" has been replaced by nearly half of the American population, and they're not sad at all—they're throwing a party and getting their war on. The Christian Right are marching to Zion with the Bush administration in one pocket and the US nuclear arsenal in the other. They've got a roadmap for the future, and it's a short one indeed.

They're determined to destroy this world in order to usher in the next. I don't know about you, but I'm a little skeptical about the veracity of their "next world." It seems to me that, despite minor inconveniences—like misquitoes and whooping cough—this world is not such a bad place, and I'm not ready to give it up without a fight. Unfortunately, that's what the Evangelical Apocalypticists have in mind, and the battle lines are being drawn even as you read this. So just how doomed are we?

NOTES

1   www.bushwatch.com, 3/16/03.

2   *Village Voice,* 5/18/04.

3   For more on the history of apocalyptic thought, its ancient roots and its effect on contemporary Christianity, see Norman Cohn's *Cosmos, Chaos and the World to Come: The Ancient Roots of Apocalyptic Faith* (Yale University Press, 2001).

4   It is ironic indeed that we do not seem to learn from history. Why do people consider their current crises to be somehow more severe than those well-documented in history, many of which were far worse? Humans have short memories, and what people are going through in the present always seems worse than what happened to other people in other times. True believers always want God to intercede for them against their enemies, and the fact that affluent, empowered Evangelicals feel so oppressed is only evidence that the Gospel has rendered them no remedy against the obsessive, narcissistic self-interest so rampant in every other aspect of American culture.

5   For more on the rising affluence amongst Evangelicals, see "We're in the Money! How did evangelicals get so wealthy, and what has it done to us?" by Michael S. Hamilton (www.christianitytoday.com/ct/2000/007/1.36.html).

6   Evangelicals have assembled a patchwork collection of unrelated Bible verses to construct their "roadmap" to the future. There are an uncountable number of books that outline this "roadmap," the first and most famous being Hal Lindsey's *The Late Great Planet Earth* (originally published in 1970, now available in a 1998 edition from Zondervan) to the latest explication by those gurus of the apocalypse, Tim LaHay and Jerry B. Jenkins, *Are We Living in the End Times?: Current Events Foretold in Scripture...and What They Mean* (Tyndale, 1999). For a liberal Christian refutation of this view, see *The*

Rapture Exposed: The Message of Hope in the Book of Revelation, by Barbara R. Rossing (Westview Press, 2005).

www.ingramcontent.com/pod-product-compliance
Lightning Source LLC
Chambersburg PA
CBHW032052080426
42733CB00006B/247